A PICTORIAL ENCYCLOPEDIA OF
THE ORIENTAL ARTS

A PICTORIAL ENCYCLOPEDIA OF
THE ORIENTAL ARTS

japan
volume 1

pre-historic period — THE NARA period (C.3rdB.C—793A.D)

edited by KADOKAWA SHOTEN

CROWN PUBLISHERS, INC. NEW YORK

A PICTORIAL ENCYCLOPEDIA OF THE ORIENTAL ARTS, compiled from the
Oriental section of the ENCYCLOPEDIA OF WORLD ART published by
Kadokawa Shoten Publishing Company, Tokyo, 1968, is published in
the United States of America, 1969 by Crown Publishers, Inc.,
419 Park Avenue South, New York, N.Y. 10016

All rights reserved
Library of Congress Catalog Card Number: 70-93408
A PICTORIAL ENCYCLOPEDIA OF THE ORIENTAL ARTS © 1969 by Crown
Publishers, Inc., New York and by Kadokawa Shoten Publishing
Company, Tokyo

Published simultaneously in Canada by General Publishing Company
Limited

The following scholars shared the editing as indicated
below:

      THE PRE-HISTORIC PERIOD   by Takiguchi Shūzō
      THE ASUKA AND HAKUHŌ PERIODS   by Fukuyama Toshio
      THE NARA PERIOD   by Noma Seiroku

Printed in Japan

Table of Contents

List of Plates — 7

Text

    The Pre-Historic Period (3rd Century B.C.—551 A.D.) — 17

    The Asuka & Hakuhō Periods (552—709 A.D.) — 23

    The Nara Period (710—793 A.D.) — 27

Glossary — 32

Table of Plates

    The Pre-Historic Period — 33
        Color Plates 1–30
        Gravure Plates 1–56

    The Asuka & Hakuhō Periods — 120
        Color Plates 31–60
        Gravure Plates 57–111

    The Nara Period — 208
        Color Plates 61–90
        Gravure Plates 112–168

LIST OF PLATES

The Pre-Historic Period

COLOR PLATES

1. Group of stones arranged in form of sundial. (Excavated from Ōyu, Akita.) Late Jōmon Period. (Special historical relic.)
2. Urn with blaze design. Excavated from Umataka, Niigata. Jōmon-type earthenware (the oldest type found in Japan, made at low temperatures with strong line patterns for decoration). Mid-Jōmon Period.
3. Jar with projecting lip. Excavated from Ōyu, Akita. Jōmon-type earthenware. $4^3/_4$ in. in height. Mid-Jōmon Period. Archaeological seminar, Meiji University, Tokyo.
4. Urn with handles. Excavated from Takikubo, Tokyo. Jōmon-type earthenware. 14 in. in height, $7^1/_3$ in. in maximum diameter. Mid-Jōmon Period. Cultural Museum, Kokubunji, Tokyo.
5. Small jar, red-colored. Excavated from Kosenzuka, Kanagawa. Jōmon-type earthenware. 3 in. in height. Late Jōmon Period. National Museum, Tokyo.
6. Small jar, vermilion-lacquered. Excavated from Kamegaoka, Aomori. Jōmon-type earthenware. $3^2/_3$ in. in height, 4 in. in maximum diameter. End Jōmon Period. Archaeological seminar, Keio University, Tokyo.
7. Clay figurine with face in shape of heart. Excavated from Gōhara, Gumma. $12^1/_4$ in. in height, $4^3/_4$–6 in. in width. Late Jōmon Period.
8. Clay figurine with face in shape of owl. Excavated from Shimpuku-ji Temple, Saitama. Late Jōmon Period. (Important cultural property.)
9. Clay figurine in crouched form. Excavated from Higashi-yuno, Fukushima. $8^1/_2$ in. in height. Late Jōmon Period.
10. Clay figurine with crown-shaped hair. Excavated from Ebisudagakoi, Miyagi. $14^1/_4$ in. in height, $8^2/_3$ in. in width. End Jōmon Period. Archaeological seminar, Tōhoku University, Sendai.
11. Clay figurine with hair in chignon. Excavated from Kamafuchi, Yamagata. 9 in. in height. End Jōmon Period. Shogen-ji Temple, Yamagata.
12. Jar, red-colored. Excavated from Matsugaseko, Fukuoka. Yayoi-type earthenware (came after Jōmon type, made at higher temperatures with more refined shape, so named after the location of its discovery, Yayoi-town, Tokyo). $8^1/_4$ in. in height, $7^3/_4$ in. in width, $4^1/_2$ in. in diameter. Mid-Yayoi Period. National Museum, Tokyo.
13. Jar, red-colored. Excavated from Takakura, Nagoya. Yayoi-type earthenware. $9^1/_2$ in. in height. Mid-Yayoi Period. National Museum, Tokyo.
14. Jar with head. Excavated from Osakata, Ibaragi. Yayoi-type earthenware. $27^1/_3$ in. in height. Mid-Yayoi Period. National Museum, Tokyo.
15. Clay figurine, inside hollow. Excavated from Kami-nojiri, Fukushima. $7^1/_2$ in. in height. Mid-Yayoi Period.
16. *Dōtaku* (bell-shaped bronze) with design of whirlpools. Excavated from Uzumori, Hyōgo. $18^2/_3$ in. in height. Mid-Yayoi Period. National Museum, Tokyo.
17. *Dōtaku* (bell-shaped bronze) with design of crossing bands. Excavated from Akugaya, Shizuoka. $25^1/_4$ in. in height. Late Yayoi Period. National Museum, Tokyo.
18. Mirror with design of human figures in Chinese type. $7^3/_4$ in. in diameter. Mid-Tumuli Period. Sumida-hachiman Shrine, Wakayama. (National treasure.)
19. Helmet with design of animals. Excavated from Gion tomb, Chiba. Gilt-bronze. $8^1/_4$ in. in height. Mid-Tumuli Period. National Museum, Tokyo.
20. Horse trappings with design of arabesque. Excavated from Oyahara tomb, Shizuoka. Gilt-

bronze. 3–3½ in. in width. Late Tumuli Period. National Museum, Tokyo.
21. Stone plate with four legs. Excavated from Maruyama tomb, Okayama. 5 in. in height. Mid-Tumuli Period. National Museum, Tokyo.
22. Figure of woman with crossing bands. Excavated from Kamishiba, Gumma. *Haniwa* (clay figurines). 11¼ in. in height. Late Tumuli Period. National Museum, Tokyo.
23. Figure of seated man. Excavated from Takahisa tomb, Fukushima. *Haniwa* (clay figurines). 35¾ in. in height. Late Tumuli Period. Iwaki High School, Fukushima. (Important cultural property.)
24. Figure of water fowl. Excavated from Saitama. *Haniwa* (clay figurines). 33¼ in. in height. Late Tumuli Period.
25. Figure of bearded man. Excavated from Himezuka tomb, Chiba. *Haniwa* (clay figurines). 54½ in. in height. Late Tumuli Period. Shibayama Haniwa Museum, Chiba.
26. Jar with decoration. *Sue*–type earthenware (made at a temperature of around 1,200°C with no glaze). Excavated from Oku-gōri, Okayama. 15¾ in. in height. Late Tumuli Period.
27. Wall painting with concentric circles. Hinōka tomb, Fukuoka. 708⅔ × 826¾ in. Late Tumuli Period. (Historical relic.)
28. Wall painting with human figure and horse. Takehara tomb, Fukuoka. Late Tumuli Period. (Historical relic.)
29. Wall painting with boat. Mezurashi-zuka tomb, Fukuoka. 807 × 531½ in. Late Tumuli Period. (Historical relic.)
30. Wall painting with horses. Ōzuka tomb, Fukuoka. Late Tumuli Period. (Special historical relic.)

GRAVURE PLATES

1. Urn with stamped patterns. Excavated from Unoki, Niigata. Jōmon-type earthenware (oldest type found in Japan, fired at low temperatures with strawrope patterns for decoration). 9¼ in. in height. Beginning Jōmon Period. Municipal Science Museum, Nagaoka, Niigata.
2. Urn with edges in shape of mountains. Excavated from Futatsugi, Chiba. Jōmon-type earthenware. 13⅓ in. in height, 9⅔ in. in mouth diameter. Early Jōmon Period. Nanzan University, Nagoya.
3. Urn, cylinder-shaped. Excavated from Fukuda, Aomori. Jōmon-type earthenware. 10⅔ in. in height. Early Jōmon Period. Nakui Agricultural High School, Aomori.
4. Bowl with snake handle. Excavated from Fudasawa, Nagano. Jōmon-type earthenware. 6½ in. in height, 9½ in. in mouth diameter, 3½ in. in bottom diameter. Mid-Jōmon Period. Municipal Museum, Nagano.
5. Urn with design of stirrups. Excavated from Asahi, Toyama. Jōmon-type earthenware. 13¾ in. in height. Mid-Jōmon Period. Anthropological Seminar, Tokyo University, Tokyo.
6. Bowl with whirlpool and oblique line designs. Excavated from Okadaira, Ibaragi. Jōmon type earthenware. 5¼ in. in height, 8¼ in. in diameter. Late Jōmon Period. Anthropological Seminar, Tokyo University, Tokyo.
7. Clay vessel with strange holes. Excavated from Shimpuku-ji Temple, Saitama. Jōmon-type earthenware. 4 in. in height. Late Jōmon Period. Anthropological Seminar, Tokyo University, Tokyo.
8. Earthen earrings. Excavated from Shinano-sakai, Nagano. Jōmon-type earthenware. 3⅓ in. in mouth diameter, 2⅓ in. in minimum diameter. Late and End Jōmon Period. Municipal Museum, Nagano.
9. Clay figurine with animal features. Excavated from Kami-kurokoma, Yamanashi. 10 in. in height. Mid-Jōmon Period. National Museum, Tokyo.
10. Stone with arabesque design. Excavated from Aba, Miyagi. 5¾ × 4 × 1⅓ in. End Jōmon Period.
11. Wooden spatula with relief curving. Excavated from Korekawa, Aomori. 20½ × ¼ in. End Jōmon Period.
12. Symbolic clay figurine. Excavated from Chōjaga-hara, Niigata. 11¾ in. in height. Mid-

13. Realistic clay figurine. Excavated from Ebara-dai, Chiba. $4^{3}/_{4}$ in. in height. Late Jōmon Period. Archaeological Museum, Meiji University, Tokyo.
14. Clay figurine with exaggerated legs. Excavated from Tokomai, Aomori. $7^{3}/_{4}$ in. in height. End Jōmon Period. National Museum, Tokyo. (Important art object.)
15. Heads of clay figurine. Excavated from Sakai, Yamanashi. $2^{3}/_{4}$ in. in height. Mid-Jōmon Period. Relic's Museum, Sakai, Yamanashi.
16. Clay figurine with exaggerated nose. Excavated from Umataka, Niigata. 7 in. in height. Mid-Jōmon Period. Municipal Science Museum, Nagaoka, Niigata.
17. Fragment of jar with design of human face. Excavated from Tsukimitai, Aomori. Jōmon-type earthenware. $6^{1}/_{3}$ in. in height. End Jōmon Period.
18. Clay figurine with exaggerated features. Excavated from Kamegaoka, Aomori. $13^{2}/_{3}$ in. in height. End Jōmon Period. (Important cultural property.)
19. Clay figurine with strange features. Excavated from Miyanoshita, Nagano. $2^{3}/_{4}$ in. in height. Mid-Jōmon Period. Anthropological Seminar, Tokyo University, Tokyo.
20. Clay figurine wearing mask. Excavated from Takaishi, Chiba. $7^{3}/_{3}$ in. in height. End Jōmon Period. Municipal Art Museum, Osaka.
21. Clay figurine in shape of vessel. Excavated from Nakayashiki, Kanagawa. $10^{1}/_{2}$ in. in height. End Jōmon Period. (Important art object.)
22. Clay figurine in shape of vessel. Excavated from Koshigoe, Nagano. $14^{1}/_{3}$ in. in height. End Jōmon Period. National Museum, Tokyo.
23. Earthen monkey. Excavated from Totsurasa, Aomori. 4 in. in height. End Jōmon Period. Anthropological Seminar, Tokyo University, Tokyo.
24. Jar with design of herringbones. Excavated from Fujisaki, Fukuoka. Yayoi-type earthenware. $7^{1}/_{2}$ in. in height, $4^{2}/_{3}$ in. in mouth diameter, 8 in. in diameter. Early Yayoi Period. Faculty of literature, Kyūshū University, Fukuoka.
25. Jar with design of horizontally terraced body. Excavated from Iwato-mura, Miyazaki. Earthenware. $9^{1}/_{4}$ in. in height. Mid-Yayoi Period. National Museum, Tokyo.
26. Jar with tall neck, red-colored. Excavated from Itazuke, Fukuoka. Yayoi type (earthenware after Jōmon type, fired at higher temperatures with more refined shape, so named after the location of its discovery, Yayoi-town, Tokyo). $11^{3}/_{4}$ in. in height. Mid-Yayoi Period. Fukuoka High School, Fukuoka.
27. Bowl, red-colored. Excavated from Mizuho, Nagoya. Yayoi-type earthenware. $9^{1}/_{3}$ in. in height. Mid-Yayoi Period. National Museum, Tokyo.
28. Ewer with openwork. Excavated from Arazawa, Nara. Yayoi-type earthenware. $8^{2}/_{3}$ in. in height, $3^{3}/_{4}$ in. in mouth diameter, $5^{2}/_{3}$ in. in diameter. Mid-Yayoi Period. Yamato Historical Museum, Nara.
29. Jar with design of vertical lines. Excavated from Funabashi, Osaka. Yayoi-type earthenware. $8^{1}/_{2}$ in. in height. Mid-Yayoi Period.
30. Globular jar. Excavated from Kugahara, Tokyo. Yayoi-type earthenware. $14^{1}/_{3}$ in. in height. Mid-Yayoi Period.
31. Tall jar. Excavated from Iwabitsu-yama. Yayoi-type earthenware. $20^{3}/_{4} \times 9$ in. $6^{1}/_{2}$ in. in diameter. Mid-Yayoi Period. National Museum, Tokyo.
32. Boating people drawing on jar. Excavated from Karako, Nara. 11 in. in height (jar), $2^{1}/_{3}$ in. in height (figure). Mid-Yayoi Period. Faculty of literature, Kyoto University, Kyoto.
33. Metal fittings for belt, with design of dragons. Excavated from Kokuzuka, Kyoto. Bronze. 4 in. in length. Late Tumuli Period. National Museum, Tokyo.
34. *Dōtaku* (bell-shaped bronze) with design of deer and stream. Excavated from Kehi, Hyōgo. $17^{3}/_{4}$ in. in height. Mid-Yayoi Period. National Museum, Tokyo. (Important cultural property.)
35. *Dōtaku* (bell-shaped bronze) with design of newt and snapping turtle. Reportedly excavated from Kagawa. $16^{3}/_{4}$ in. in height. Mid-Yayoi Period. (National treasure.)
36. Bronze mirror with design of hunting scenes. Excavated from Hachiman-hara, Gumma. $7^{1}/_{4}$ in. in height. Early Tumuli Period. National Museum, Tokyo. (Important cultural property.)
37. Bronze mirror with design of animals. Excavation area unknown. $15^{1}/_{4}$ in. in diameter. Early Tumuli Period. National Museum, Tokyo. (Important cultural property.)
38. Figure of large house. Excavated from Saitobaru tomb, Miyazaki. *Haniwa* (clay figurine).

2 in. in height. Mid-Tumuli Period. National Museum, Tokyo. (Important cultural property.)

39. Figure of boat. Excavated from Saitobaru tomb, Miyazaki. *Haniwa* (clay figurine). $39^3/_4$ in. in length. Mid-Tumuli Period. National Museum, Tokyo. (Important cultural property.)
40. Figure of man wearing *hakama* (pleated skirt). Excavated from Enkō-ji Temple, Okayama. *Haniwa* (clay figurine). $32^1/_2$ in. in height. Late Tumuli Period.
41. Figure of woman holding up hands. Excavated from Gumma. *Haniwa* (clay figurine). $28^3/_4$ in. in height. Late Tumuli Period.
42. Figure of warrior. Excavated from Kugo, Gumma. *Haniwa* (clay figurine). $52^1/_3$ in. in height. Late Tumuli Period. National Museum, Tokyo. (Important cultural property.)
43. Figure of man playing *koto* (musical instrument). Excavated from Asakura, Gumma. *Haniwa* (clay figurine). $28^2/_3$ in. in height. Late Tumuli Period. Archaeological Museum, Aikawa, Gumma. (Important cultural property.)
44. Figure of falconer. Excavated from Fuchina, Gumma. *Haniwa* (clay figurine). $29^1/_3$ in. in height. Late Tumuli Period. (Important cultural property.)
45. Figure of seated man. Excavated from Hachimanhara, Gumma. *Haniwa* (clay figurine). Late Tumuli Period. Tenri Sankō-kan Museum, Nara. (Important cultural property.)
46. Figure of woman. Excavated from Himezuka tomb, Chiba. *Haniwa* (clay figurine). $34^1/_3$ in. in height. Late Tumuli Period. Shibayama Haniwa Museum, Chiba.
47. Figure of nursemaid. Excavated from Torizuka tomb, Tochigi. *Haniwa* (clay figurine). $16^1/_3$ in. in height. Late Tumuli Period. National Museum, Tokyo.
48. Figure of monkey. Excavated from Okisu, Ibaragi. *Haniwa* (clay figurine). $10^3/_4$ in. in height. Late Tumuli Period. (Important cultural property.)
49. Figure of warrior. Excavated from Himezuka tomb, Chiba. *Haniwa* (clay figurine). $6^1/_3$ in. in height. Late Tumuli Period. Shibayama Haniwa Museum, Chiba.
50. Figure of wild boar. Excavated from Kamitakeshi, Gumma. *Haniwa* (clay figurine). 20 in. in height. Late Tumuli Period. National Museum, Tokyo. (Important cultural property.)
51. Figure of horse with trapping. Excavated from Shiraishi, Gumma. *Haniwa* (clay figurine). 46 in. in height. Late Tumuli Period. National Museum, Tokyo.
52. Figure of farmer. Excavated from Akabori-mura, Gumma. *Haniwa* (clay figurine). $36^1/_4$ in. in height. Late Tumuli Period. National Museum, Tokyo.
53. Figure of dancing people. Excavated from Nohara, Saitama. *Haniwa* (clay figurine). $25^1/_4$ in. in height (left), $22^1/_4$ in. in height (right). Late Tumuli Period. National Museum, Tokyo.
54. Jar on foot decorated with human figures. *Sue*-type earthenware (fired at temperature of around 1,200°C with no glaze). Excavated from Nishimiyayama tomb, Hyōgo. $14^3/_4$ in. in height. Late Tumuli Period. National Museum, Kyoto.
55. A. Jar with design of man carrying load on shoulders (detail of No. 54).
    B. Jar with design of wrestling (detail of No. 102).
56. Cinerary coffin. Pottery with design of man leading horse in relief curving. Excavated from Hirafukuyama tomb, Okayama. $33^3/_4$ in. in height. Late Tumuli Period. National Museum, Tokyo.

The Asuka and Hakuhō Periods

COLOR PLATES

31. Kannon (Avalokitesvara), known as "Kudara Kannon." Wood. $82^1/_3$ in. in height. 7th century. Hōryū-ji Temple, Nara. (National treasure.)
32. Jikoku Ten (Dhrtarastra), one of four guardian kings. Wood. $52^3/_4$ in. in height. 7th century. Golden Hall, Hōryū-ji Temple, Nara.
33. Yakushi (Bhaisajya-guru). Bronze. $24^3/_4$ in. in height. 607 A.D. Golden Hall, Hōryū-ji Temple, Nara. (National treasure.)
34. Miroku (Maitreya). Wood. $48^2/_3$ in. in height. 7th century. Kōryū-ji Temple, Kyoto. (National treasure.)
35. Bodhisattva (one of "Six Kannon"). Wood. $33^3/_4$ in. in height. 7th century. Hōryū-ji Temple, Nara.
36. Lady Maya (mother of Sakyamuni Buddha) and heavenly beings. Bronze. $6^1/_2$ in. in height.

7th century. National Museum, Tokyo (originally in Hōryū-ji Temple).

37. Shaka (Sakyamuni) and two attendants. Bronze. 14 in. in height. 7th–8th century. National Museum, Tokyo (originally in Hōryū-ji Temple).
38. Amida (Amitabha) and two attendants, placed in Lady Tachibana's Shrine. Bronze. $13\frac{1}{4}$ in. in height. Second half of 7th – early 8th century. Hōryū-ji Temple, Nara. (National treasure.)
39. Miroku (Maitreya). Clay. $87\frac{3}{4}$ in. in height. Late 7th – early 8th century. Golden Hall, Taimadera Temple, Nara. (National treasure.)
40. Head of Yakushi (Bhaisajya-guru). Bronze. Late 7th – early 8th century. Golden Hall, Yakushi-ji Temple, Nara. (National treasure.)
41. Relief on pedestal of Yakushi (Bhaisajya-guru) (detail). Bronze. Second half of 7th – early 8th century. Golden Hall, Yakushi-ji Temple, Nara.
42. Shaka (Sakyamuni) and two attendants. Stone. $27\frac{1}{4}$ in. in height. Second half of 7th century. Ishii-dera Temple, Nara.
43. Bodhisattvas, painted on door of Tamamushi Shrine. Color on wood. $12\frac{1}{3} \times 7\frac{2}{3}$ in. 7th century. Hōryū-ji Temple, Nara.
44. Jātaka scene (a prince, later the Buddha, laying down his life to hear the sacred verses). Color on wood. Painted on pedestal of Tamamushi Shrine. $25\frac{2}{3} \times 14$ in. 7th century. Hōryū-ji Temple, Nara.
45. Jātaka scene (a prince, later the Buddha, sacrificing himself to feed a hungry tigress and her cubs). Painted on pedestal of Tamamushi Shrine. Color on wood. 7th century. Hōryū-ji Temple, Nara.
46. Painting on pedestal of Lady Tachibana's Shrine. Color on wood. Second half of 7th – early 8th century. Hōryū-ji Temple, Nara.
47. Painting on pedestal of Lady Tachibana's Shrine. Color on wood. $21\frac{2}{3} \times 20$ in. Late 7th – early 8th century. Hōryū-ji Temple, Nara.
48. Bodhisattva (Wall No. 2). Mural in Golden Hall. Color on white washed wall. $123\frac{2}{3} \times 60\frac{1}{4}$ in. Late 7th – early 8th century. Hōryū-ji Temple, Nara. (Important cultural property.)
49. Heavenly maidens in flight. Mural in Golden Hall (small wall near ceiling of inner sanctuary). Color on whitewashed wall. $29\frac{3}{4} \times 54\frac{3}{4}$ in. Late 7th – early 8th century. Hōryū-ji Temple, Nara. (Important cultural property.)
50. Bodhisattva and attendants (Wall No. 10, detail). Mural in Golden Hall. Color on white-washed wall. $123\frac{1}{4} \times 100\frac{1}{3}$ in. Second half of 7th – early 8th century. Hōryū-ji Temple, Nara. (Important cultural property.)
51. Bodhisattva (Wall No. 6, detail). Mural in Golden Hall. Color on whitewashed wall. $122\frac{3}{4} \times 102\frac{1}{3}$ in. Late 7th – early 8th century. Hōryū-ji Temple, Nara. (Important cultural property.)
52. Prince Shōtoku. Color on paper. $49\frac{1}{4} \times 20$ in. Late 7th – early 8th century. (Imperial collection.)
53. Main Sanctuary (Honden). $35\frac{3}{4}$ ft. square. Rebuilt in 1744 A.D. Izumo-taisha Shrine, Shimane. (National treasure.)
54. Five-storied Pagoda. $35\frac{2}{3}$ ft. square. $106\frac{1}{2}$ ft. in height. 7th century. Hōryū-ji Temple, Nara. (National treasure.)
55. Golden Hall (Kondō). $60\frac{1}{3}$ (front) × $49\frac{3}{4}$ ft. (side). 7th century. Hōryū-ji Temple, Nara. (National treasure.)
56. Interior of Golden Hall. Hōryū-ji Temple, Nara.
57. Sacred casket, originally installed in the lost pagoda of Shūfuku-ji Temple. Glass, gold, silver and bronze. 11 in. in height (right), 3 in. in height (left). Late 7th century. Ōmi-jingū Shrine, Ōtsu. (National treasure.)
58. Gargoyle. Excavated from the precinct of Yakushi-ji Temple, Nara. Tile. $15\frac{1}{4} \times 17\frac{1}{2} \times 2\text{-}2\frac{3}{4}$ in. 7th century. Anonymous collection, Kyoto.
59. *Gigaku* (ancient mask play) mask, "Chidō" (for the first performance role). Wood. $11\frac{1}{2}$ in. in height. 7th century. National Museum, Tokyo (originally in Hōryū-ji Temple).
60. Embroidered picture of Tenjukoku Paradise (detail). Silk. $34\frac{3}{4} \times 32\frac{1}{2}$ in. About 622 A.D. Chūgū-ji Temple, Nara. (National treasure.)

GRAVURE PLATES

57. Shaka (Shakyamuni) and two attendants. Bronze. 34 in. in height (Shaka), 35³/₄ in. in height (attendants). 623 A.D. Golden Hall, Hōryū-ji Temple, Nara. (National treasure.)
58.59. Kannon (Avalokitesvara), known as "Kudara Kannon." Wood. 82¹/₃ in. in height. 7th century. Hōryū-ji Temple, Nara. (National treasure.)
60.61. Kannon (Avalokitesvara), known as "Guze Kannon." Wood. 77¹/₂ in. in height. First half of 7th century. Yumedono Hall, Hōryū-ji Temple, Nara. (National treasure.)
62. Tamon Ten (Vaisravana), one of four guardian kings. Wood. 52¹/₃ in. in height. 7th century. Golden Hall, Hōryū-ji Temple, Nara.
63. Zōjyō Ten (Virudhaka), one of four guardian kings. Wood. 52¹/₂ in. in height. 7th century. Golden Hall, Hōryū-ji Temple, Nara.
64. Figure of phoenix attached to canopy. Wood. 11³/₄ in. in height. 7th century. Golden Hall, Hōryū-ji Temple, Nara.
65. Figure of heavenly maiden attached to canopy. Wood. 6²/₃ in. in height. 7th century. Golden Hall, Hōryū-ji Temple, Nara. (National treasure.)
66. Kannon (Avalokitesvara), known as "Yumetagai Kannon." Bronze. 33³/₄ in. in height. Late 7th–early 8th century. Hōryū-ji Temple, Nara. (National treasure.)
67. Bodhisattva (one of "Six Kannon"). Wood. 33³/₄ in. in height. Late 7th century. Hōryū-ji Temple, Nara. (Important cultural property.)
68. Scene of Buddha's nirvana. Clay. 711 A.D. Five-storied Pagoda, Hōryū-ji Temple, Nara.
69.70. Weeping disciples at Buddha's nirvana. Clay. 18¹/₂ in. in height (69), 18¹/₄ in. in height (70). 711 A.D. Five-storied Pagoda, Hōryū-ji Temple, Nara.
71. Head of Buddha. Bronze. 42 in. in height. 685 A.D. Kōfuku-ji Temple, Nara. (Important cultural property.)
72. Woman in scene of Monju and Yuima (disciples) discussing Buddhism. Clay. 15¹/₄ in. in height. 711 A.D. Five-storied Pagoda, Hōryū-ji Temple, Nara.
73. Miroku (Maitreya). Wood. 52¹/₃ in. in height. 7th century. Chūgū-ji Temple, Nara. (National treasure.)
74. Bodhisattva, called Kokūzō (Akasagarbha). Wood. 69¹/₂ in. in height. 7th century. Hōrin-ji Temple, Nara. (Important cultural property.)
75. Miroku (Maitreya), known as "Hōkan (crowned) Miroku." Wood. 48²/₃ in. in height. 7th century. Kōryū-ji Temple, Kyoto. (National treasure.)
76. Miroku (Maitreya), known as "Naki (weeping) Miroku." Wood. 39²/₃ in. in height. 7th century. Kōryū-ji Temple, Nara. (National treasure.)
77. Yakushi (Bhaisajya-guru). Bronze. 100¹/₃ in. in height. Second half of 7th–early 8th century. Golden Hall, Yakushi-ji Temple, Nara.
78. Pedestal of Yakushi (detail). Bronze. Second half of 7th–early 8th century. Golden Hall, Yakushi-ji Temple, Nara.
79.80. Shō Kannon (Avalokitesvara). Bronze. 74³/₄ in. in height. Second half of 7th century. Yakushi-ji Temple, Nara. (National treasure.)
81.82. Heavenly being (part of top-ornament of East Pagoda). Bronze. 74³/₄ × 19²/₃ in. 690–730 A.D. Yakushi-ji Temple, Nara. (National treasure.)
83. Shaka (Sakyamuni). Bronze. 32¹/₄ in. in height. Second half of 7th – first half of 8th century. Jindai-ji Temple, Tokyo. (Important cultural property.)
84. Bodhisattva, called Shō Kannon (Avalokitesvara). Wood. 20 in. in height. Second half of 7th century. Konryū-ji Temple, Nara. (Important cultural property.)
85. Lady Maya (mother of Sakyamuni). Bronze. 6¹/₂ in. in height. 7th century. National Museum, Tokyo.
86. Miroku (Maitreya). Bronze. 15¹/₄ in. in height. 7th century. National Museum, Tokyo. (Important cultural property.)
87.88 Figures of men. Stone. 47¹/₄ in. in height. 7th century. Tomb of Princess Kibi, Nara.
89. Bodhisattva, painted on side door of Lady Tachibana's shrine. Color on wood. Late 7th–early 8th century. Hōryū-ji Temple, Nara.
90. Kannon (Wall No. 6., detail). Color on whitewashed wall. 123¹/₄ × 102¹/₃ in. Mural in Golden Hall. Second half of 7th–early 8th century. Hōryū-ji Temple, Nara. (Important cultural

property.)
91. Bodhisattva (Wall No. 5., detail). Mural in Golden Hall. Color on whitewashed wall. $123^{1}/_{4} \times$ 59 in. Second half of 7th–early 8th century. Hōryū-ji Temple, Nara.
92. Amida (Amitabha)(Wall No. 6., detail). Mural in Golden Hall. Color on whitewashed wall. $123^{1}/_{4} \times 102^{1}/_{3}$ in. Second half of 7th–early 8th century. Hōryū-ji Temple, Nara.
93. Kannon (Avalokitesvara) (Wall No. 3). Mural in Golden Hall. Color on whitewashed wall. $123^{1}/_{4} \times 62^{1}/_{4}$ in. Second half of 7th–early 8th century. Hōryū-ji Temple, Nara. (Important cultural property.)
94. Heavenly maiden in flight. Fun drawing on canopy. Ink on wood. 7th century. Golden Hall, Hōryū-ji Temple, Nara.
95. Boy. Fun drawing on ceiling board. Ink on wood. $3 \times 2^{2}/_{3}$ in. 7th century. Five-storied Pagoda, Hōryū-ji Temple, Nara.
96. Faces of two men. Fun drawing on ceiling board. Ink on wood. $2^{3}/_{4} \times 2^{1}/_{3}$ in. 7th century. Golden Hall, Hōryū-ji Temple, Nara.
97. 98. Five-storied Pagoda. $35^{2}/_{3}$ ft. square. $106^{1}/_{2}$ ft. in height. 7th century. Hōryū-ji Temple, Nara. (National treasure.)
99. Chūmon (inner main gateway). $39^{1}/_{3}$ ft. (front), 28 ft. (sides). 7th century. Hōryū-ji Temple, Nara. (National treasure.)
100. Corridor of Hōryū-ji Temple. $250^{1}/_{2}$ ft. in overall lenghth (east corridor), $238^{1}/_{2}$ ft. in overall length (west corridor). 7th century. Hōryū-ji Temple, Nara. (National treasure.)
101. 102. Niō (Vajrapani), two door-guardians. Clay. 130 in. in height. 711 A.D. Inner main gateway, Hōryū-ji Temple, Nara. (Important cultural property.)
103. Three-storied Pagoda. $21^{1}/_{3}$ ft. square. $78^{1}/_{2}$ ft. in height. 7th century. Hokki-ji Temple, Nara. (National treasure).
104. Ceiling of East Pagoda. $9^{1}/_{2}$ in. square (one section). 690–730 A.D. Yakushi-ji Temple, Nara.
105. Seiden (main sanctuary). 441 in. (front), $212^{2}/_{3}$ in. (sides). Rebuilt in 1953. Kōdai-jingū Shrine, Ise.
106. Honden (main sanctuary). $187^{1}/_{3}$ in. (front), 313 in. (sides). Rebuilt in 1804. Sumiyoshi-taisha Shrine, Osaka. (National treasure.)
107. 108. Fragments of embroidered picture of Tenjukoku (paradise) (detail). Silk. $34^{3}/_{4} \times 32^{1}/_{2}$ in. About 622 A.D. Chūgū-ji Temple, Nara.
109. 110. Canopy (detail). Wood. 7th century. Golden Hall, Hōryū-ji Temple, Nara. (National treasure.)
111. Figure of heavenly maiden. Relief on slab. $15^{1}/_{3} \times 15 \times 3^{1}/_{4}$ in. 8th century. Oka-dera Temple, Nara. (Important cultural property.)

The Nara Period

COLOR PLATES

61. Mekira (Mihira), one of twelve guardians of Yakushi. Clay. $5^{1}/_{2}$ ft. in height. 729–748 A.D. Shin Yakushi-ji Temple, Nara. (National treasure.)
62. Gakkō Bosatsu (Candraprabha). Clay. $81^{1}/_{3}$ in. in height. First half of 8th century. Sangatsu-dō Hall, Tōdai-ji Temple, Nara. (National treasure.)
63. Shikkongō Shin (Vajrapani). Clay. 66 in. in height. 733 A.D. Sangatsu-dō Hall, Tōdai-ji Temple, Nara. (National treasure.)
64. Ashura (Asura), one of eight supernatural guardians of Shaka. Dry-lacquer. $60^{1}/_{4}$ in. in height. 734 A.D. Kōfuku-ji Temple, Nara. (National treasure.)
65. Shubodai (Subhuti), one of the ten great disciples of Shaka. Dry-lacquer. 58 in. in height. About 734 A.D. Kōfuku-ji Temple, Nara. (National treasure.)
66. Priest Gyōshin. Dry-lacquer. $35^{1}/_{4}$ in. in height. 8th century. Yumedono Hall, Hōryū-ji Temple, Nara. (National treasure.)
67. Jikoku Ten (Dhrtarastra), one of four guardian kings. Clay. $63^{1}/_{4}$ in. in height. First half of 8th century. Kaidan-in, Tōdai-ji Temple, Nara. (National treasure.)
68. Gigei Ten (Goddess of Arts). Head. Dry-lacquer. $83^{1}/_{2}$ in. in height. Second half of 8th

century. Akishino-dera Temple, Nara. (Important cultural property.)
69. Priest Ganjin. Dry-lacquer. 31$^2/_3$ in. in height. About 763 A.D. Founder's Hall, Tōshōdai-ji Temple, Nara. (National treasure.)
70. Head of Bodhisattva. Dry-lacquer. 24 in. in height. Second half of 8th century. Tōshōdai-ji Temple, Nara. (Important cultural property.)
71. *Gigaku* (ancient mask drama) mask, "Karura" (man-bird). Wood. 11$^3/_4$ in. in height, 8 in. in width. Mid-8th century. Tōdai-ji Temple, Nara. (Important cultural property.)
72. Heavenly musician, on one of the panels of octagonal lantern fire-chamber (detail). Bronze. 36$^3/_4$ in. in height, 17$^1/_3$ in. in width. Mid-8th century. In front of Great Buddha Hall, Tōdai-ji Temple, Nara. (National treasure.)
73. Figure playing music on elephant, painted on plectrum guard of *biwa* (lute). Color on leather. 16 in. in length, 6$^1/_2$ in. in width. 8th century. Shōsō-in Temple Repository, Nara.
74. Bodhisattva painted on sanctuary pillar. Color on wood. 763–764 A.D. Octagonal Hall, Eizan-ji Temple, Nara. (National treasure.)
75. Hokkedō Kompon Mandala, showing Shaka (Sakyamuni) preaching at vulture peak (detail). Color on silk. 42$^1/_4$ × 56$^1/_4$ in. 8th century. Museum of Fine Arts, Boston.
76. Lady under tree (one panel of a folding screen) (detail). Ink and slight color on paper (orignally decorated with bird-down). 53$^1/_2$ × 22 in. 8th century. Shōsō-in Temple Repository, Nara.
77. Kichijō Ten (Mahasri) (detail). Color on ramie. 21 × 12$^2/_3$ in. 772 A.D. Yakushi-ji Temple, Nara. (National treasure.)
78. Illustrated Inga-kyō Sutra (detail). Color on paper. 10 × 4 in. 8th century. Jōbonrendai-ji Temple, Kyoto. (National treasure.)
79. Sangatsu-dō Hall (detail). 57 ft. (front), 82$^1/_4$ ft. (sides). 740–750 A.D. Tōdai-ji Temple, Nara. (National treasure.)
80. Yume-dono Hall. 15$^1/_3$ ft. in length (each side). 8th century. Hōryū-ji Temple, Nara. (National treasure.)
81. Yume-dono Hall and surmounting ornament. Copper. 8th century. Hōryū-ji Temple, Nara. (National treasure.)
82. Interior of Dempō-dō Hall. 82 ft. (front), 35 ft. (sides). 730–750 A.D. Hōryū-ji Temple, Nara. (National treasure.)
83. Treasure Repository (detail). 108$^2/_3$ ft. (front), 25 ft. (sides). 750–760 A.D. Shōsō-in Temple, Nara.
84. Octagonal Hall. 33$^1/_4$ ft. in height, 10$^3/_4$ ft. in length (each side). 8th century. Eizan-ji Temple, Gojo. (National treasure.)
85. Hand-roll folders. Knit bamboo with patterned-weave silk hems. 19$^2/_3$ in. in length, 12 in. in width. 8th century. Shōsō-in Temple Repository, Nara.
86. Ritual banner with design of peacock. Embroidery. 8th century. Shōsō–in Temple Repository, Nara.
87. Cloth with design of hunting scene. Weft-patterned *nishiki* (colorful weave) silk. 8th century. Shōsō-in Temple Repository, Nara.
88. Bronze mirror. Back design of flowers, birds and animals. Back lacquered with inlaid mother-of-pearl. 15$^1/_2$ in. in diameter, $^1/_2$ in. in thickness. 8th century. Shōsō-in Temple Repository, Nara.
89. Octagonal box. Tortoise shell over wood, with mother-of-pearl inlay. 15$^1/_2$ in. in diameter, 5 in. in height, 6 in. (each side). 8th century. Shōsō-in Temple Repository, Nara.
90. Five-stringed *biwa* (lute) (detail). Red sandalwood with mother-of-pearl inlay. 42$^3/_4$ in. in length, 12 in. in width, 3$^1/_3$ in. in thickness. 8th century. Shōsō-in Temple Repository, Nara.

GRAVURE PLATES

112. Ashura (Asura), one of eight supernatural guardians of Shaka. Dry-lacquer. 60$^1/_4$ in. in height. About 734 A.D. Kōfuku-ji Temple, Nara. (National treasure.)
113. 114. Shubodai (Subhuti), one of ten great disciples of Shaka. Dry-lacquer. 57$^3/_4$ in. in height. About 734 A.D. Kōfuku-ji Temple, Nara. (National treasure.)

115. Nikkō Bosatsu (Surya-prabhasa). Clay. 81³/₄ in. in height. First half of 8th century. Sangatsu-dō Hall, Tōdai-ji Temple, Nara. (National treasure.)
116. Gakkō Bosatsu (Gandraprabha). Clay. 81¹/₃ in. in height. First half of 8th century. Sangatsu-dō Hall, Tōdai-ji Temple, Nara. (National treasure.)
117. Kōmoku Ten (Virupaksa), one of four guardian kings. Clay. 64¹/₃ in. in height. First half of 8th century. Kaidan-in Monastery, Tōdai-ji Temple, Nara.
118. Zōjyō Ten (Virudhaka), one of four guardian kings. Clay. 64¹/₃ in. in height. First half of 8th century. Kaidan-in Monastery, Tōdai-ji Temple, Nara.
119. Kichijō Ten (Mahasri) (detail). 79¹/₂ in. in height. Second half of 8th century. Sangatsu-dō Hall, Tōdai-ji Temple, Nara. (Important cultural property.)
120. Fukū Kensaku Kannon, Nikkō Bosatsu and Gakkō Bosatsu in Sangatsu-dō Hall, Tōdai-ji Temple, Nara.
121. Kongō Rikishi (close-mouthed one of pair). Dry-lacquer. 134³/₄ in. in height. Mid-8th century. Sangatsu-dō Hall, Tōdai-ji Temple, Nara. (National treasure.)
122. Zōjyō Ten (Virudhaka), one of four guardian kings (detail). Dry-lacquer. 119¹/₃ in. in height. Mid-8th century. Sangatsu-dō Hall, Tōdai-ji Temple, Nara.
123. Anera Taishō (Anila), one of twelve guardians of Yakushi. Clay. 65²/₃ in. in height. 729–748 A.D. Shin Yakushi-ji Temple, Nara. (National treasure).
124. Basara Taishō (Vajra), one of twelve guardians of Yakushi. Clay. 64¹/₃ in. in height. 729–748 A.D. Shin Yakushi-ji Temple, Nara.
125. Eleven-headed Kannon (Avalokitesvara). Dry-lacquer. 82¹/₄ in. in height. Second half of 8th century. Shōrin-ji Temple, Nara. (National treasure.)
126. Shaka (Sakyamuni). Dry-lacquer. 28¹/₃ in. in height. Second half of 8th century. Saidai-ji Temple, Nara. (Important cultural property).
127. Priest Gyōshin. Dry-lacquer. 35 in. in height. 8th century. Yume-dono Hall, Hōryū-ji Temple, Nara. (National treasure.)
128. Nikkō (Surya-prabhasa) (detail). Dry-lacquer. 22 in. in height. Second half of 8th century. National Museum, Tokyo. (originally in Kōzan-ji Temple, Kyoto). (Important cultural property.)
129. Rushana (Vairocana) (detail). Dry-lacquer. 119¹/₃ in. in height. 759 A.D. Golden Hall, Tōshōdai-ji Temple, Nara. (National treasure.)
130. Thousand-arm Kannon (Avalokitesvara). Dry-lacquer. 211 in. in height. Second half of 8th century. Golden Hall, Tōshōdai-ji Temple, Nara. (National treasure).
131. Bon Ten (Brahma). Wood. 75 in. in height. Second half of 8th century. Golden Hall, Tōshōdai-ji Temple, Nara. (National treasure.)
132. Taishaku Ten (Gakradevanum Indra). Wood. 74¹/₃ in. in height. Second half of 8th century. Golden Hall, Tōshōdai-ji Temple, Nara.
133. Jikoku Ten (Dhrtarstra), one of four guardian kings. Wood. 59¹/₂ in. in height. Second half of 8th century. Daian-ji Temple, Nara.
134. Tamon Ten (Vaisravana), one of four guardian kings. Wood. 55²/₃ in. in height. Second half of 8th century. Daian-ji Temple, Nara.
135. *Gigaku* (ancient mask drama) mask, "Suikojyū" (for drunken attendant roles). Wood. 13 × 9¹/₂ in. 8th century. Tōdai-ji Temple, Nara. (Important cultural property.)
136. *Gigaku* (ancient mask drama) mask, "Gojyo" (for young woman roles). Wood. 9 × 6³/₄ in. 8th century. Shōsō-in Repository, Nara.
137. Illustrated Inga-kyō Sutra (detail, showing Prince Siddharta going through palace gate). Color on paper. 10 × 407³/₄ in. 8th century. Jōbonrendai-ji Temple, Kyoto. (National treasure.)
138. 139. Lady under tree (detail). Panel of folding-screen. Ink and faint color on paper (originally decorated with bird-down). 53¹/₂ × 22 in. 8th century. Shōsō-in Repository, Nara.
140. Bodhisattva (detail). Ink on ramie. 54¹/₂ × 52¹/₃ in. 8th century. Shōsō-in Repository, Nara.
141. Bodhisattva, painted on ritual banner (detail). Color on silk. 8th century. Shōsō-in Repository, Nara.
142. Design of sacred animal (detail). Faint color on paper. 8th century. Shōsō-in Temple Repository, Nara.
143. Landscape (detail). Ink on ramie. 23 × 70 in. 8th century. Shōsō-in Temple Repository, Nara.
144. Birds with flowering branches in beaks, painted on tray (detail). Litharge color on lacquered

wood. 15$\frac{1}{3}$ in. in diameter, 2 in. in height. 8th century. Shōsō-in Temple Repository, Nara.
145. Painting on tray. Litharge color on lacquered wood. 15$\frac{1}{3}$ in. in diameter, 1$\frac{3}{4}$ in. in height. 8th century. Shōsō-in Temple Repository, Nara.
146. East Gateway of Hōryū-ji Temple. 370 in. (front), 211$\frac{1}{2}$ in. (sides), 420 in. in height. 8th century. Hōryū-ji Temple, Nara. (National treasure.)
147. Sutra Repository. 362$\frac{2}{3}$ in. (front), 199$\frac{2}{3}$ in. (sides), 411$\frac{1}{2}$ in. in height. 8th century. Hōryū-ji Temple, Nara. (National treasure.)
148. Lecture Hall. 1330$\frac{2}{3}$ in. (front), 532$\frac{1}{4}$ in. (sides). 708–15 A.D. Tōshōdai-ji Temple, Nara. (National treasure.)
149. Golden Hall. 1102$\frac{1}{3}$ in. (front), 576$\frac{3}{4}$ in. (sides). Second half of 8th century. Tōshōdai-ji Temple, Nara. (National treasure.)
150. Crown of Fukū Kensaku Kannon. Silver with jeweled pendants. 19 in. in diameter, 22$\frac{2}{3}$ in. in height. 746 A.D. Sangatsu-dō Hall, Tōdai-ji Temple. Nara. (National treasure.)
151. Buddhist ritual banner (detail). Gilt bronze. 67 in. in length. 17 × 6 in. (one section). 8th century. Shōsō-in Temple Repository, Nara.
152. Jar. Silver. 17 in. in diameter, 18$\frac{1}{3}$ in. in height. 8th century. Shōsō-in Temple Repository, Nara.
153. Incense burner. Copper. 9$\frac{1}{2}$ in. in diameter. 8th century. Shōsō-in Temple Repository, Nara.
154. Cabinet. Black persimmon wood. 20$\frac{1}{2}$ × 25$\frac{3}{4}$ × 13$\frac{2}{3}$ in. 8th century. Shōsō-in Temple Repository, Nara.
155. Cabinet, Red-lacquered. Zelkova wood. 39$\frac{1}{3}$ × 33 × 16 in. 8th century. Shōsō-in Temple Repository, Nara.
156. Rectangular box. Wood, with marquetry in betel-nut palm wood. 4$\frac{1}{3}$ × 13 × 9$\frac{1}{4}$ in. 8th century. Shōsō-in Repository, Nara.
157. Box. Wood, decorated with gold and silver ornament on green priming and overlaid with tortoise shell. 6$\frac{1}{4}$ × 21$\frac{1}{4}$ × 21 in. 8th century. Shōsō-in Temple Repository, Nara.
158. Box. Wood, decorated with gold and silver on green priming. 4 × 11 × 7 in. 8th century. Shōsō-in Temple Repository, Nara.
159. Eight-lobed mirror box. Lacquered hide with gold and silver painting. 8$\frac{1}{4}$ in. in diameter, 13$\frac{3}{4}$ in. in height. 8th century. Shōsō-in Temple Repository, Nara.
160. Eight-lobed mirror box. Wood, lacquered with silver inlay. 14$\frac{1}{3}$ in. in diameter, 4$\frac{1}{4}$ in. in height. 8th century. Shōsō-in Temple Repository, Nara.
161. *Biwa* (lute) (back side). Red sandalwood, inlaid with mother-of-pearl, amber and tortoise shell. 38$\frac{3}{4}$ in. in length, 16 in. in mouth diameter. 8th century. Shōsō-in Repository, Nara.
162. Foot measures. Green-stained ivory with engravings. Plectrum (*Bachi*, right). Red-stained ivory with engravings. 8th century. Shōsō-in Temple Repository, Nara.
163. Eight-lobed mirror. Bronze, covered with silver. Design of landscape. 16 in. in diameter, $\frac{1}{2}$ in. in thickness. 8th century. Shōsō-in Temple Repository, Nara.
164. Octagonal mirror box. Wood, covered with brocade. 17$\frac{3}{4}$ in. in diameter, 1$\frac{1}{2}$ in. in thickness. 8th century. Shōsō-in Temple Repository, Nara.
165. Bowl. Two-color glazed pottery. 8$\frac{2}{3}$ in. in minimum diameter, 9$\frac{3}{4}$ in. mouth diameter. 8th century. Shōsō-in Temple Repository, Nara.
166. Dish. Two-color glazed pottery. 14$\frac{3}{4}$ in. in diameter, 2 in. height. 8th century. Shōsō-in Repository, Nara.
167. Vase. Two-color glazed pottery. 7 in. in mouth diameter, 7 in. in bottom diameter, 42 in. in height. 8th century. Shōsō-in Temple Repository, Nara.
168. Knives with rhinoceros-horn hilt and silver scabbord, decorated with jewels. Blade, 3$\frac{1}{3}$ in. in length, scabbord, 4$\frac{3}{4}$ in. in length, and hilt, 3$\frac{1}{2}$ in. in length. 8th century. Shōsō-in Temple Repository, Nara.

JAPAN

The Pre-Historic Period

It was probably late in the Paleolithic Age, near the end of the Diluvial Epoch, tens of thousands of years ago, that man began to inhabit the Japanese Archipelago. Simple stone implements are the sole artifacts of this earliest Japanese culture, still largely unknown to us.

The Jōmon Period

The first rudimentary plastic art appeared in Japan during the Jōmon period. People who previously had produced only simple stone implements learned a new technique: making earthenware of fired clay. This earliest Japanese earthenware is termed Jōmon (cord-mark) pottery, and the period of some thousand years until the second or third century B.C. is called the Jōmon period. Jōmon period man had not mastered agriculture and had no metal implements. He depended on hunting and fishing for sustenance and used stone, bone, or horn tools. The many stone arrowheads discovered from this period prove that bow-and-arrow hunting was already known. The use of archery and earthenware seems to indicate a greatly enriched diet. Once freed from a never-ending search for food, Jōmon period men gained spare time with which to ornament their tools, and thus created primitive decorative arts. The main artifacts of the Jōmon period are handicrafts such as pottery and personal ornaments, sculptures such as *dogū* (clay figurines), and decorative handles of earthenware vessels. Pictorial art is almost nonexistent.

Jōmon people settled where they could easily obtain food from sea and land. Their abodes were pit-houses, level-ground houses, or sometimes caves. The pit-house was a form of dwelling also used in the later Yayoi and Kofun periods. It consisted of a rectangular, round, or oval hollow dug in the ground, a few pillars, and a roof. A deeper, smaller hollow for fires was dug in a part of the floor. Although its basic plan is known, its superstructure, for example the construction of the roof, can only be imagined.

Jōmon pottery is so termed because of the characteristic cord or rope marks decorating its surface. A vessel was built up by coiling a rope of clay and was finished by pressing a cord or cords against the surface of the soft paste before firing. Twisting the cord in various ways, or using it wound around a wooden pin, created different patterns. The surface was decorated not only by impressing cords, but also by such methods as rolling wooden pins with carved patterns across it, by stroking the vessel with a comb, or by pressing the clay with the edge of a scalloped shell or the end of a bamboo stem — a whole stem to form circles, a split stem to form semicircles. Repeating or combining these designs created a variety of attractive ornamental patterns.

Jōmon pottery was in use for several thousand years. Shapes and ornamentation naturally vary in different epochs and localities. Most popular during Jōmon's first stage were deep, cannonball-shaped bowls with pointed bases. These bowls are decorated either with Jōmon patterns formed by twisted cords or wooden pins wound with cords, with linear patterns created with shells, or with stamped patterns made by carved wooden pins. Shapes in the second stage of Jōmon pottery-making are characterized by flat bases. Cord-mark ornament, originally developed in eastern Japan, was disseminated into western Japan, and bamboo-stem marks reappeared. Notable changes took place in the third, or middle stage, of Jōmon. One notes in particular that large, thick-walled urns and deep bowls with decorative spirals, waves, and other curvilinear designs appeared in the area from the southern part of the Kantō area to the mountainous region of Chūbu. We find remarkable works of art made of clay decorated with sculptural ornaments — such as molded projections recalling flames, human or animal masks, or snakes — applied to the rim of the pot's mouth and to its handles. Vessels from this epoch decorated with this three-dimensional ornamentation are probably the most ornate Jōmon pottery. The impressive, heavy shapes and ornaments reflect the enormous vigor of people who fought with nature and dared to migrate into mountain regions.

Jōmon pottery changed extensively after this peak period; notably, its shapes diversified according to function. Urns, large and small bowls, vessels with spouts and/or tall legs, and so on, came into wide use, while purely decorative vessels also proliferated. Curved and spiraled ornamentation tended to be replaced by neat engraved lines. Delicate decorative effects were achieved by new techniques — decorating the entire surface with cord-marks and then rubbing off part of them, or keeping certain areas of the surface undecorated. A smoothly polished surface, or one painted with the red ocher characteristic of this period, contrasts markedly with the three-dimensional ornaments of the middle epoch.

The forms and ornaments of *dogū* (clay figurines) show developments similar to those of Jōmon pottery. At first the clay figurines were flat triangles with barely suggestive heads, arms, and breasts. Standing figures were first fashioned in the middle stage of the Jōmon period. The faces, frequently reminiscent of monstrous animals, were far from human and often quite grotesque. Most figures have protruding breasts, and some specimens represent pregnant women. Clay figurines from the late Jōmon to the early Yayoi periods include a few of a stable hollow shape containing the bones of babies. The use of these bizarre relics is unknown.

The purpose of *dogū* has been explained in various ways, so far inconclusively. They may have been magical objects connected with procreation or fertility, or religious tokens believed to draw illnesses onto themselves. Stone figurines (*gangū*), clay plaques (*doban*), stone plaques (*ganban*), and clay masks (*domen*) are thought to be varieties of *dogū*.

The esthetic sense of the Jōmon people is manifested best in their personal designs. Wild boars, deer, and other animals provided them with meat and with bones, horns and teeth suitable for various ornaments. Antlers offered a suitable material for hair ornaments, waist pendants, and other minutely carved baubles. Ornaments for pierced ears were usually made of clay. They are almost always circles, often decorated with pierced work or with red paint. Ear ornaments as well as pendants were sometimes made of jadite, though no one has yet explained how Jōmon people could work the hard jadeite without metal tools.

The Yayoi Period

The period following the Jōmon period, from the second or third century B.C. to about the third century A.D., is called the Yayoi period. Continental culture strongly influenced this period, and notable progress was made in all aspects of social life. The most important landmarks were the importation of the bronze and iron cultures, and the beginning of agriculture. The latter encouraged a settled life centered around rice paddies, and led eventually to the emergence of communities. Bronze weapons such as swords, spears, and halberds were imported to the area situated nearest the Asian Continent around northern Kyūshū. Surviving molds are evidence that such bronze objects were also manufactured in Japan. Bronzes of a strange shape known as *dōtaku* (bronze bells) were cast in the Kinki district in central Japan. Metal culture was unknown in the eastern regions from the Kantō district northward, however, where the Jōmon culture was still thriving. Developments in the Yayoi period were thus restricted primarily to western Japan.

Contrasting with that of Jōmon, earthenware of the Yayoi period is a light-brown ware, often polished and painted with red ocher. Its forms are simple and smart, with little or no surface decoration. The most common shapes are jars for storage, urns for cooking, and tall-footed vessels and bowls for holding food. The method of manufacture differed little from that of Jōmon pottery, but a primitive type of wheel seems to have been in use. Differences among localities and epochs are not pronounced, though some specimens from the northern Kantō and Tōhoku districts, the eastern half of Japan, retain cord-mark patterns from the Jōmon period and have their mouth rims decorated with human masks. Among earthenware from the Kinki district are some line-engraved objects with primitive pictures of human figures, deer, birds, boats or houses, noteworthy as embryonic works of pictorial art.

Casting bronze was one of the crafts which began in this period. Specimens include edged tools, mirrors, bracelets, and *dōtaku*. *Dōtaku* are peculiar to Japan and are the most distinctive bronze objects of the Yayoi period. Ranging in height between about ten centimeters (four inches) and one hundred centimeters or more, they are in slightly tapered cylindrical forms with flattened sides. They resemble hanging bells, but their purpose has not been explained satisfactorily. The probable explanation is that they were suspended percussion instruments that later became ceremonial objects placed on the ground at agricultural rituals. *Dōtaku* have two vertical flanges, or fins, along opposite rims, and a semicircular band on the top. They are classified into two main types by their surface ornamentation: one type has sequences of water-streams (parallel curving lines); the other has vertical and horizontal bands sectioning the surface into four or six panels. Both sides are decorated with zigzags, herringbones, continuous spirals, and other geometric motifs. The panels bordered by crossed bands and part of the stream-patterned surface are often decorated further with line-relief designs such as fern-frond patterns, human and animal figures, and houses. These designs are related to the primitive pictures often traced on the surface of earthenware objects. Duplicates cast from the same mold have been discovered at widely different sites. Probably they were made by expert craftsmen and distributed to various localities.

The Kofun Period

A unified nation with its center in the Kinai area (the area covering the present Nara, Kyoto, and Osaka) was established at the end of the third or beginning of the fourth century following the Yayoi period. Huge tombs covered with tumuli were built for dignitaries. The Kofun (ancient tombs or tumuli) period denotes an age lasting until about 646 A.D., when an Imperial order was issued prohibiting overly luxurious interment rites and when the custom of cremation was introduced. Kofun tombs varied in ground plan, with most being round, square, or keyhole-shaped. The keyhole type is a unique Japanese form. Recent studies have proven that the dimensions of the front angular part and the rear circular part were designed according to set principles. Various treasures were buried in the stone burial chambers of the tombs as funerary offerings. The magnificent engineering work of building the tombs, the splendid works of decorative arts buried in them, and the paintings ornamenting the walls of the burial chambers provide noteworthy relics of the Kofun period.

The technique of bronze casting was carried over from the Yayoi period, and the Kofun period witnessed a substantial production of cast-bronze mirrors. Mirror-back ornaments at first imitated their Chinese equivalents, depicting immortals, mystic animals, and the like. Later, unique Japanese designs were also created: geometric patterns composed of combinations of straight lines and arcs believed to have had some magical meaning; graphic designs showing hunting scenes, houses, and so forth; and even mirrors with bells attached to their rims.

Relations with Korea, which had increased since about the fifth century, introduced various pieces of arms and armor, personal ornaments such as crowns, shoes, ear pendants, belt plaques, and horse trappings. Korean craftsmen also came to Japan; consequently decorative arts in gold, silver, and gilt bronze developed rapidly. The surviving specimens display every conceivable technique of metalworking: casting, carving, openwork, line engraving, gilding, and inlay. Ornamental motifs include not only the traditional dragons and floral scrolls but also such designs as tortoiseshell (hexagons) and animals.

Maga-tama (curving or claw-shaped beads) of jadite, *kuda-dama* (cylindrical beads) of jasper, and *maga-tama* and *maru-dama* (globular beads) of glass had been used during the Yayoi period. Beads of the Kofun period are made of a great assortment of materials including amber, rock crystal, and agate, and their shapes show richer variety. Jasper was also used for bracelets, small covered boxes, footed vessels, and other objects.

The main types of earthenware in the Kofun period are Haji pottery derived from Yayoi pottery, and Sue pottery, made by a new technique introduced from Paekche in southern Korea. Sue is a high-fired, hard, dark gray or medium gray ware, fashioned on the potter's wheel and fired at at least 1,000 degrees centigrade. It contains a considerable range of shapes. Predominating in the first half of the sixth century are jars with sculptured ornaments — fully rounded human figures, animals, diminutive jars, and so on. The figures, related in some features to Haniwa figures, attract us by their wonderful expression of movement and their simplicity.

Haniwa are terra-cotta objects placed on tumuli. They are of two kinds: barrel-shaped, cylindrical haniwa with two or three hooplike bands of clay applied to them; and representational haniwa, models of such objects as houses, boats, arms and armor, hats, *kinugasa* (long-shafted baldachins held over dignitaries), and of animals and men. The cylindrical shape is earliest. Haniwa houses, shields, *kinugasa*, and such were first made in the Kinai area about the middle of the fourth century, and animal and human figures toward the end of the fourth or early in the fifth century. When these representational haniwa were erected on a tumulus, they were arranged in a square right above the burial chamber as if to surround it.

A change took place during the sixth and seventh centuries. Haniwa figures were no longer made in Kinai, but were produced in enormous quantities in the Kantō district of eastern Japan. They also became more diversified in form. Human figures represented not only people connected with the ruling classes, such as ceremonial functionaries, warriors clad in armor, and priestesses, but also commoners in everyday settings: a couple dancing, a mother carrying her baby on her back, a peasant carrying a hoe across his shoulder and a sickle at his waist. Animal figures also abound: a monkey with its head tilted and turned, a chicken pecking, and so on.

Representational haniwa were often set up on one side of a tumulus, near the entrance to the burial chamber, or in a square some distance from the tomb. Haniwa cylinders also were sometimes arranged in triple circles around the top, middle, and base of the tumulus, probably to serve as fences bordering a sacred ground. This leads us to believe that haniwa were at first objects for funeral rites, and later became more ornamental than functional. The naive, bright, and often noble expressions of haniwa figures impress us with the vitality and emotional richness of these early Japanese. Stone sculptures of human figures (*sekijin*) and horses (*sekiba*) have been found in northern Kyūshū. They were also erected as ornaments at tombs, and are regarded to be a local variation of haniwa.

From the Asian Continent men learned in the second half of the fifth century to build a new type of tomb. This tomb had a stone burial chamber entered at ground level on one side. The chamber was constructed with large slabs and blocks of stone; its walls and the stone coffin placed in it were often decorated with line engravings or color paintings. Tombs so decorated are found chiefly in northern Kyūshū, but relatively simple ones of a later date are scattered throughout other districts. Early decorations were geometric motifs line engraved or carved in relief on stone coffins. Later, these ornaments were painted in color, and subsequently developed into color murals free from carving. The coloring, from natural mineral pigments, always includes red, and may include yellow, white, blue, green, or black. The main motifs are geometric patterns (straight lines and arcs, triangles, circles, and fern fronds), man-made objects (arms and armor, boats, and houses), and figures of men, birds, and beasts. Geometric motifs probably preceded graphic ones.

The practice of decorating the interior of a burial chamber with color paintings of human figures, horses, and abstract shapes may have been inspired by wall paintings in Korean tombs of the Koryo Dynasty (fifth century). Ornamenting a stone coffin with carved geometric motifs, however, was a purely Japanese idea; we cannot ascribe the origin of decorated tombs in Japan solely to Continental influence. Whatever their inspiration, the decorated tombs in northern Kyūshū, ranging in date between the second half of the fifth century to the ninth century, contain important specimens of Japanese murals prior to the famous wall paintings in the main hall of the Hōryū-ji Temple in Nara.

During its course of development from Jōmon through Yayoi to the Kofun period, ancient Japanese culture was strongly influenced by that of the Asiatic Continent. The Japanese harmonized the traditional with the foreign to create new phases of culture, and so prepared for the blooming of Buddhist culture in the forthcoming periods.

The Asuka and Hakuhō Periods

Buddhism was introduced into Japan about the middle of the sixth century. Its introduction marked an epoch in the history of Japanese art for it brought with it architecture, sculpture, painting, and handicrafts of a totally new kind. Engineers and architects, as well as painters, sculptors, and experts in various other fields, came to Japan one after another from the Korean Peninsula. When Buddhism reached Japan, it was both an agglomeration of highly advanced technical crafts, and a rich and well-established international culture extending over India, China, and Southeast Asia.

Buddhist culture rooted itself deeply in the Yamato area (the present Nara Prefecture), which was the political center of the country. Buddhist icons and the temples needed to house them were soon created in this area, opening a new chapter in the history of Japanese art. This first epoch, covering about a century after the introduction of Buddhism, is termed the Asuka period.

The first part of the Asuka period overlaps the last part of the preceding Kofun period, the Protohistoric Age. Although the imported foreign culture represented by Buddhism flourished, so did the tradition of Protohistoric culture. Japan's older forms of artistic expression were still actively alive. Vestiges of these coexisting cultures can be noted even in the districts in which administration and culture were centered. Kofun period culture clearly dominated areas far removed from the capital.

Buddhism and Buddhist culture were absorbed eagerly by the Japanese of the time. It is of course hard to tell how well they understood the religious doctrines of Buddhism, or the religious significance of statues of Buddhist deities. We may imagine, however, that their ardent absorption of Buddhism was motivated by their interest in its advanced, widespread culture.

Korean cultural influences had been strong in Japan before the Yamato Court was established in the fourth century. Gradually culture imported from Korea alone was felt to be insufficient. By the sixth century, Japan had begun to send envoys and Buddhist monks directly to China to study Buddhist culture there. As a result, Japanese art of the Asuka period was permeated throughout with the inspiration of Chinese arts of the Six Dynasties period (222–589), the period preceding the Sui and T'ang Dynasties.

Absorption of the more advanced Chinese culture prompted innovation in government, too. Various regulations were created touching the central and local governments, the military, police and travel, and such matters of civil administration as family registration and farm lands. A taxation system, regulating payment of taxes in goods or labor, was also established. The administrative structure of the country, centered around the Imperial Court, was gradually consolidated, until finally the written law known as the Taihō Ritsuryō (Statute of the Taihō Era), based on Chinese law, was established at the beginning of the eighth century.

Japan followed this statute system stressing centralized power for many centuries.

Meanwhile, communication with China became more frequent than ever. Many students and Buddhist monks visited China, then under the T'ang Dynasty, and brought back Chinese ideas and artifacts. The influence of T'ang art thus was first felt around the middle of the seventh century, and was disseminated widely thereafter. Art historians call this the Hakuhō period.

It may be seen from the above that influence from Chinese culture accumulated to help form Japanese culture. In the following discussion, let us examine more concretely the arts of the Asuka and Hakuhō periods.

Buddhism brought many wonders with it. The most surprising to the Japanese must have been Buddhist architecture with its towering pagodas and magnificent buildings with their red pillars and tiled roofs. This architecture must indeed have awed people who lived in houses with thatched roofs and *hottate* pillars (pillars with their bases buried in the ground instead of resting on foundation stones). The carpenters, tile makers, metalworkers, and other artisans who came to Japan in 588 A.D. from Paekche, Korea, introduced engineering techniques for building Buddhist temples with tiled roofs. The Imperial Court encouraged the construction of temples, and leading clans competed to establish their own temples. The first monumental temple born out of this social situation was the Asukadera. The plan of its temple building finds its prototype in the Koguryo and Paekche Dynasties of Korea; naturally, Korean elements abounded in this earliest temple in Japan. The most common plan for temples in this period, however, set the main hall and the pagoda in a north-south line, and it is termed the Shitennōji-type plan. It represents a Japanese modification of a Korean mode. This plan, often with variations, was used in most temples built thereafter during the Asuka period. No wooden building still exists which definitely dates from the Asuka period, but the plan of the Hōryū-ji Temple and details of its main buildings are believed to embody the architectural style of the period.

A new type of temple plan was introduced during the second half of the Hakuhō period. This type, probably brought from the Korean kingdom of Silla, featured two pagodas placed opposite each other on the east and west sides of the temple. Typical of this type is the Yakushi-ji Temple, finished about 698 A.D. Elaborate designs were created for the respective buildings of Yakushi-ji Temple, each of which was intended as a fine work of art. Its surviving pagoda (the east pagoda) represents the architectural style of the Hakuhō period and is admired as the most beautiful wooden building not only in Japan but in the world.

Surviving sculptures from the Asuka and Hakuhō periods are limited to Buddhist works. According to documentary evidence, the first Buddhist statue was brought to Japan in 538 A.D. It was a gilt bronze statue of the Buddha Shaka (Sakyamuni) and was a gift to the Japanese Imperial Court from the King of the Paekche Dynasty in Korea. The appearance of the statue is of course unknown. However, 538 A.D. was shortly after the Northern Wei Dynasty in China, later replaced by the two dynasties of Eastern and Western Wei, but the Northern Wei style still dominated Chinese sculpture. The gilt bronze statue brought from Paekche probably was in this Northern Wei style, a style which dictated Buddhist sculpture in Japan for a century. It follows that Buddhist sculpture was transmitted from China to Japan through Korea.

The Korean kingdom of Paekche sent to Japan in 577 A.D. a group of Buddhist sculptors, priests, and architectural technicians, and some copies of sutras (Buddhist scriptures). Korean sculptors must have been in wide demand. The Buddhist sculptor who best represents the Asuka period, however, is Kuratukuri no Tori, a descendant of a naturalized Chinese. Representative sculptures from this period were made mainly by Tori and his disciples. The Tori style is characterized by rigid, heavy representation, symmetrical form, large eyes and ears in clear, simple shapes, and the "archaic smile" peculiar to ancient art. This style, created by the accomplished artists of Northern Wei, continued to thrive in Japan, attesting to its popularity there.

Statues in the Tori style were cast in bronze and gold-plated. Gilt bronze was a new and fascinating medium for Japanese sculptors, previously confined to using clay, stone, or wood. Hence, a new sculptural medium also resulted from the importation of Buddhism.

The Tori style was gradually replaced in the Hakuhō period by a style of softer, more pleasant representation and bright, youthful, almost childlike expression. Tenderness and lightness became important. This change reflects the influence of the Chinese plastic sense of the early T'ang period and foreshadows the even more endearing, idealistic beauty of the Nara period.

In the century and a half after Buddhism was introduced to Japan, Japanese sculpture gradually turned from symbolic, mysterious effigies to images of ideal beings of the perceivable world. This change was of course due partly to changes in religious faith and the perception of Buddhist ideas. Nevertheless, it is remarkable that Japanese sculpture could have made such a substantial development in such a short period of time, and could have produced a number of masterworks not inferior to their Chinese and Korean models.

In the last part of the Protohistoric Age, that overlapped the Asuka period, the Japanese created a considerable number of tombs whose stone burial chambers were ornamented with colored paintings or graphic drawings. The Japanese thus were well grounded in graphic art when Buddhist painting was introduced. Ancient documents reveal that a group of artists was officially nominated in 604 A.D. to specialize in the hereditary profession of painting. Painting at the time was confined to decorating Buddhist temples. Keeping professional painters under government control helped to promote Buddhism, but it may also indicate that technical experts began to be trained under national protection. As in sculpture and other fields of art, naturalized foreigners or their descendants were the early leaders. The oldest surviving example of pictorial art from this period is the Tenjukoku Shūchō, an embroidered picture of the Tenjukoku Paradise made in 622 A.D. Certain detailed parts of this tapestry clearly reflect the Chinese style of the Six Dynasties, while the clothing of figures reveals common characteristics with that in tomb murals of the Koguryo Dynasty in Korea. This resemblance indicates the sources of Japanese techniques and technicians. Because these technicians were engaged in decorating temples, they were more distinguished in creating ornamental design than in genuine painting.

In the early Hakuhō period, it became fashionable to paint Buddhist deities and angelic figures on the walls of the main halls and pagodas of temples, since the interior of such building were believed to represent a Pure Land (Buddha Land or paradise). Painters were thus given a wider field to display their ability, as is demonstrated best in the wall paintings in the Main Hall of the Hōryū-ji Temple. Here the style of Chinese art of the early T'ang period is transplanted in its purest form, and is then polished by an even higher artistic sense. The remarkable development from the crude Tenjukoku Shūchō in the Asuka period to the glorious Hōryū-ji murals in the Hakuhō period is astonishing, especially when we consider that these great strides were taken in only a very short period in the seventh century. This rapid change evidences how eager the nation and its technicians were to assimilate Buddhist culture.

Decorative arts, being connected directly with life, found their natural expression in useful objects, as archaeological relics attest. Various tribes specializing in their respective crafts were in the service of the Imperial Court in the Kofun period (the Protohistoric Age): textile craftsmen engaged in spinning, weaving, dyeing, and sewing; metalworkers in smithery, and the manufacture of bronze mirrors and metal fittings, and so on. Armorers, woodworkers, stoneworkers, and potters manufactured all sorts of functional objects. Each time that naturalized craftsmen possessing more advanced Continental techniques joined these groups, they enriched the variety and heightened the quality of the handicrafts. The technical mastery thus attained was applied to new fields after the importation of Buddhism, mainly in the manufacture of religious ritual objects and ornaments. The technical foundation laid during archaeological times made possible the splendid flowering of handicrafts in early Buddhist culture which in some fields has never been surpassed.

One of the most noteworthy changes connected with Buddhism in the decorative arts was the introduction of designs containing international elements. To cite just one example, the metal fittings attached to the Tamamushi Shrine are embellished with beautiful openwork in a design combining half-palmate motifs in various ways. This motif probably originated in Egypt, and was polished in Greece into a dynamic continuous pattern. The completed design was transmitted to Persia and India, from where it traveled along with Buddhism through Central Asia, China, and Korea to Japan. The design thereafter formed a favorite motif of the Asuka period.

Most of the surviving specimens of decorative arts from the Asuka and Hakuhō periods are, naturally enough, metal. They show that all the techniques of metalworking we now know were already employed in those times. They furthermore manifest an astonishingly high technical level, from the casting of colossal bronze statues to the elaborate repoussé work of small metal fittings.

Surviving pieces of textile art are few, but documentary evidences suggest that sophisticated work was done in weaving, embroidery, braiding, and dyeing. Existing specimens of imported Chinese *chin* (colorfully patterned woven silk) suggest that imitation fabrics must have been woven in Japan.

Innumerable pieces of Asuka pottery and woodwork and many personal ornaments still exist. Notable among these are glass beads unearthed from building sites at temples, for they prove that such man-made gems were already used along with natural precious and semiprecious stones.

The Nara Period

The statutory system of centralized power was most forcefully active in the Nara period. Administrative organizations established during the previous period were strengthened, and efforts were devoted to the ambitious project of creating an ideal nation. The central government, focused on the Emperor, had the power to govern local districts, and secured nationwide control of the labor force, productivity, and the collection and distribution of goods. In accord with the country's new aims, the capital was transferred in 710 A.D. to a place more suitable for a permanent, large-scale center of national administration. The idea of having such a capital, and the plan of the city thus created, derived from the Chinese T'ang capital. But the change was not merely prompted by the urge to imitate a more advanced country: it must have been absolutely necessary in order to enforce governmental policy effectively. The new capital, Heijō-kyō (Heijō Capital), corresponds approximately to the present city of Nara, and the period when Heijō was the capital of the country (710–784) is called the Nara or Tempyō period.

Buddhism helped promote the new capital. Shortly after its introduction into Japan, Buddhism won popular support by promising personal rewards (the Buddha's blessing) in the present and future worlds to the faithful. Buddhism prospered under the protection of the Imperial Court and of the powerful clans, but it largely owed its success to its miraculous promises. In the Nara period, however, scriptures associated with the peace and welfare of the nation or with rich harvests received new emphasis. Buddhism tended increasingly to be a religion for the nation rather than for individuals. Naturally enough, it was patronized more eagerly than ever by a government endeavoring to stabilize its nation. The construction of the universe according to Buddhist cosmology appealed to statesmen as an ideal form for a centralized nation, and provided them with an important source of ideas on their national administrative system. Buddhism throve with the nation, and the nation prospered with Buddhism.

As a matter of necessity, the government protected Buddhist art as the visual embodiment of Buddhist concepts. Works of art produced under national direction were great in magnitude and aspiration; they reflect the vigor of a people devoted to the creation of a new nation.

Art of this period reflects clearly the willingness of the nation to assimilate T'ang culture. T'ang art is an international style merging East and West. Japanese art from the Nara period is rich in Persian, Indian, Southeast Asian, and other foreign elements.

Because Buddhism was under national protection, the construction of a

Buddhist temple was usually a national project. Temples were erected by the government, mainly in Nara, but also in the provinces. When building a new temple, an office (Zōji-shi or Temple Construction office) was temporarily organized to raise the necessary materials and manpower from local districts. All craftsmen thus conscripted were organized by their craft and incorporated into an existing governmental organization. Those already employed by various governmental offices were summoned on occasion to lend a hand on a project.

The grandest of these nationwide engineering works was the construction of the Tōdai-ji Temple to house the Great Buddha, a colossal gilt bronze statue of the Buddha Rushana (Vairocana). In 741 A.D., the Emperor Shōmu issued an Imperial order to build a Kokubun-ji Temple (Provincial Official Temple) in each province under the overall jurisdiction of Tōdai-ji Temple. According to the Buddhist cosmology of the time, each province was regarded as a minor universe centered around a Kokubun-ji Temple, and the nation was regarded as a macrocosm in which the provinces centered around the Tōdai-ji Temple. The Great Buddha provided the religious as well as secular nucleus of Japan.

Although construction work on Tōdai-ji Temple started in 745 A.D. the important buildings were not finished until near the end of the Nara period. The project was a tremendous undertaking requiring the nation's combined resources of materials and labor. The temple site covered an area of about 80,000 square meters; the Great Buddha Hall, the main building of the temple, was about eighty-six meters in length and 50.5 meters in width; the Great Buddha housed in it was almost sixteen meters high. Unfortunately, most of the original buildings have been destroyed by repeated fires, but details of the construction are known from surviving documents.

Just as construction of temples was a national project, so the production of Buddhist statues was undertaken by national institutions called Zōbutsu-sho (Offices for the Production of Buddhist Statues). Sculptors called from the various districts were assigned to the Bussho (sculptors' studio) of their office. There they were provided with materials and tools, as well as clothing and money. No famous individual sculptor can emerge from such a system, a precept which applies to other craftsmen of the period as well. Among craftsmen of the time were some of distinguished ability and some with high reputations, but all artistic activities were joint works, often involving many craftsmen.

The period witnessed a change in the materials of sculpture. Gilt bronze had been the main material in the preceding periods; the Nara period saw a vogue for clay sculpture and dry-lacquer sculpture, the latter being something like papier-mâché. A statue is made by applying many alternate layers of hemp cloth and lacquer. The change in materials may have been due partly to economic reasons, but probably occurred primarily because these plastic materials were more suitable for realistic representation.

The earliest known example of these clay sculptures is a group of statuettes made in 711 A.D. and placed on four sides of the first story of the five-storied pagoda at the Hōryū-ji Temple. Clearly showing the influence of T'ang sculpture, they are quite realistic and humanistic. This stylistic trend may be noted also in dry-lacquer sculpture, for example the Jū Dai Deshi (Ten Great Disciples of the Buddha) and the Hachi-bu-shū (Eight Supernatural Guardians of the Buddha) in the Kōfuku-ji

Temple, which were completed in 734 A. D. They are a direct translation of the T'ang style. Although they are in calm, standing poses, their faces bear very realistic expressions. Quiet standing poses are also employed in statues representing awesome, dynamic guardian deities. Examples are the Shitsukongō-shin (Vajrapani, about 733) in the Hokkedō Hall of the Tōdai-ji Temple; the Shi Tennō (Four Deva Kings) in the Kaidanin of the same temple; and the Jūni Shinshō (Twelve Heavenly Generals) in the Shin-yakushi-ji Temple, all in clay. They reveal the remarkable ability of their sculptors in plastic representation, while retaining some rigidity from the previous epoch in the treatment of their lower halves.

The clay statues in the Tōdai-ji Temple were made at the government operated Zōbutsu-sho. The most distinguished work of sculpture produced at the Zōbutsu-sho must be the Fukūkensaku Kannon (Amoghapasa, about 748) which represents the flawless culmination of Nara-period style, a style achieved through full mastery of T'ang art. Its full, dignified figure is heroic, and its face — austere but benevolent — conveys an expression of profound, lofty religious thought not seen in earlier periods.

The enormous ability and self-confidence of the Tōdai-ji Zōbutsu-sho eventually resulted in the making of the Great Buddha, the most magnificent monument in the history of Japanese sculpture, a work created through the full utilization of Japan's resources, labor, and intellect. After the completion of the Great Buddha, the Nara period enters its final phase. The last flowers of this period are the groups of wood carvings in the Tōshōdai-ji and the Daian-ji temples. These wooden statues show a plastic sense of an entirely new kind, characterized by full-cheeked faces with sullen expressions, and bulky figures with broad shoulders and amply modeled waists. They obviously reflect the influence of Chinese sculpture of the time. Perhaps they were carved by Chinese sculptors who had come to Japan. They were to inspire, in the following period, a new style of wood sculpture which went beyond mere realism.

Officially established temples enhanced their grandeur and glory steadily during the Nara period. Painters were involved in such activities as ornamenting buildings, producing wall paintings, coloring dry-lacquer and clay statues, decorating hand-copied scriptures, and executing underdrawings for designs on decorative art objects. Like other craftsmen, painters belonged to official organizations and worked in a collaboration made closer by strong teacher-pupil relationships. Their technical ability was therefore fairly uniform. Proficiency was esteemed more than individuality. Other painters were attached to temples or free-earned, but even they were called occasionally for governmental collaborative works.

We have documents describing in detail such systems and activities of these organizations of painters as their production of religious paintings in cooperation with sculptors and their coloring of finished statues. None of their works, however, still exist, except for some slight traces of ornamental patterns on statues. In the surviving examples recurs a beautiful coloring method termed *ungen saishiki* (rainbow coloring), in which flowers, tendril scrolls, flowering plants, phoenixes, and other decorative motifs were painted in parallel bands of graduated tones of a color. This method of coloring was also employed on architectural ornaments and on works of decorative art.

Little can be said about wall paintings and other large paintings of the time, as no examples survive. However, the underdrawings for the "Screen Panels of Standing Ladies Decorated with Bird's Feathers," and the lines of figures of Bodhisattvas drawn on hemp cloth, are sufficient indications that the artistic quality of Nara-period painting was superb. The use of hemp cloth as the base for paintings was due mainly to the accessibility of that material, but its use gave birth to a peculiar technique of white undercoating. A typical masterpiece in this genre is the painting owned by the Yakushi-ji Temple showing the Buddhist goddess Kichijōten (Srimahadevi). The picture dates from about 771 A.D. The beautiful, elaborate coloring of the clothing of the goddess, and the nobility of the graceful figure, are reminiscent of Chinese figure painting of the T'ang period. It shows a neater composition and more advanced technique than the "Screen Panels of Standing Ladies," and tends to favor a soft, delicate style.

Decorative arts of the Nara period are known through the numerous art treasures preserved in the Shōsō-in Temple in Nara. The works of art collected there epitomize the world-wide Buddhist cultural sphere of the time. They cover a wide assortment of objects: household goods, musical instruments, costumes for musicians and dancers, articles for amusement, personal ornaments, textiles, dinnerware, Buddhist ritual objects, and many other treasures. There are remarkable works of art in metal, wood, lacquer, ivory, textiles, and ceramics, displaying a superb command of materials and a technical mastery.

It is generally agreed that only part of the Shōsō-in treasures were made in Japan. Many are believed to have been brought from China or even more distant parts of the world, and international elements merge beautifully in them. For example, there are musical instruments decorated with designs of elephants, camels, and other animals and plants of southern regions, and screens and vessels painted with pictures in Sassanid Persian style. Shapes of receptacles include some of Persian origin which were in favor in China. These foreign rarities were brought from various parts of the world along the famous Silk Road to Changan, the capital of T'ang China. They were subsequently transmitted to Japan through trade with China.

Nara craftsmen not only created remarkable shapes and designs, but many of their techniques have never been surpassed. One example is *heidatsu*, otherwise known as *hyōmon*, a technique of lacquer art in which very thin plates of gold or silver are cut into desired shapes and embedded into an object's surface. The entire surface is then coated with lacquer, and finally the lacquer is removed from the inlaid part. This technique was developed in this period and attained astonishing precision and elaborateness. Notable technical development was also made in various other fields, such as mother-of-pearl inlay, marquetry, hairline engraving, cloisonné, embroidery, *nishiki* (polychrome patterned weaving), *kyōkechi* (dyeing by inserting the cloth between two perforated boards and pouring the dye stuff through the perforations), *rōkechi* (batik), glasswork, and casting and other metal-art crafts. The varying materials and techniques were combined in flawless harmony to create exquisite works of decorative arts.

Although it must be admitted that many of these splendid pieces were imported and were owned by only a few patricians, we can imagine that Japanese craftsmen provided with these wonderful samples of technique endeavored to rival their makers. A conspicuous example can be noted in ceramics. Japanese potters who had heretofore manufactured only primitive earthenware were inspired by the beautiful glazed pottery of China called Tō Sansai (T'ang three-colored ware) to create a ware approximating it, known as Nara Sansai, specimens of which are included in the Shōsō-in Temple. Possibly, the Shōsō-in treasures contain many more Japanese works than is generally believed.

Glossary

Asukadera : The first Buddhist temple erected in Japan (end of the sixth century). The temple is not standing today but is thought to have been in the style of Paekche (Korea) temples.

dōgū : Clay figurines, usually between three and ten inches high.

dōtaku : Bronze, bell-like objects peculiar to Japan. They are representative art objects of the Yayoi Period. Their exact use is uncertain.

haji **pottery** : An unglazed, reddish-brown pottery derived basically from *yayoi* pottery. It was used for ordinary everyday purposes in the Kofun Period.

haniwa : Reddish-brown or terracotta clay objects excavated from fourth and fifth century tumuli. *Haniwa* were believed to placate the spirit of the deceased, and to serve the deceased in afterlife.

Heijō-kyō : The capital of Japan for seventy years of the eighth century. Heijō corresponds roughly to an area stretching north from present-day Nara. Many temples were built in the capital, making it not only the political but also the religious center of the period.

Hōryū-ji : A temple built in Nara in the seventh century. It is the world's oldest extant wooden structure, and houses a number of Buddhist images that represent the finest in Japanese art.

jōmon **style** : The oldest pottery found in Japan. Made of clay, *jōmon* pottery is unglazed and fired at low temperatures. The name comes from its distinctive cord-marking (*jōmon*) decorations. The pottery gives its name to the period from 4–3000 B.C. to 1000 B.C.

Kofun Period : The period from the third century to the seventh century, during which large-scale tumuli (kofun) were constructed. The main tumuli were in mound or keyhole shapes. Wall frescoes in the tombs were either patterns, or paintings depicting myths.

Kuratsukuri no Tori : A famous sculptor of the early seventh century (Asuka period). He received commissions from Prince Shōtoku and effected many outstanding Buddhist images in the Northern Wei style.

magatama : Curved or claw-shaped beads usually made of glass, rock crystal, amber or agate. They were used for body ornamentation.

nishiki : A weaving method which uses many different colors of thread to create colorful patterns. The technique was introduced to Japan in the sixth and seventh centuries from China and Korea.

sansai : Literally "three colors," *sansai* refers to three-colored, glazed pottery, the most famous of which comes from T'ang China. Nara *sansai*, dating from the Nara period, approximates the T'ang *sansai*.

sekijin : Human figures of stone found in northern Kyūshū and dating from the middle of fifth century. Horse and other animal figures are also found, sometimes together with *haniwa*.

Shitennō-ji : One of seven famous temples built between the sixth and seventh centuries by Prince Shōtoku. Its name designates the type of temple construction that places the Main Hall and the Pagoda in a north-south line.

Shōsō-in : Though originally part of Tōdai-ji Temple of the Nara period, Shōsō-in today is a veritable treasure house of Japanese and imported art from all periods of history. It preserves not only a wide variety of Buddhist art and utility objects but also armor, musical instruments, wearing apparel, medicines, cooking ware, and a host of other articles.

sue **pottery** : Colored dark or medium gray, *sue* pottery was extremely hard, and fired at high temperatures. It was a product of highly advanced techniques introduced to Japan in late Kofun from Paekche in Korea.

Tōdai-ji : The largest wooden structure in the world. The temple was built in the Nara period but the Main Hall—which has the large Buddha image—is an Edo period reconstruction.

ungen saishiki : A coloring method, begun in the Nara period, which employed graduated tones of a single color in parallel bands. Two such colors were generally used together, leaving the viewer with an extremely vivid impression. It was used for coloring Buddhist images, paintings and for decorating temples. The only examples remaining today are on some Buddhist images.

Yakushi-ji : Constructed at the end of the seventh century, Yakushi-ji is a representative temple of the Hakuhō period.

yayoi **style** : Pottery that appeared in Japan after *jōmon*. The name derives from the Yayoi section of Tokyo where the pottery was first excavated in 1868. The period during which this was used—from the second or third century B.C. to the third century A.D.—is called the Yayoi Period.

Pre-historic Period

1 Group of stones arranged in form of sun-dial. Late Jōmon Period.

3 Jar with projecting lip, Jōmon Type Earthenware. Late Jōmon Period.

2 Urn with blaze design, Jōmon Type Earthenware. Mid-Jōmon Period.

4 Urn with handles, Jōmon Type Earthenware. Mid-Jōmon Period.

5 Small jar, red-coloured, Jōmon Type Earthenware. Late Jōmon Period.

6 Small jar, vermilion-lacquered, Jōmon Type Earthenware. End Jōmon Period.

7 Clay figurine with face in shape of heart. Late Jōmon Period.

8 Clay figurine with face
  in shape of owl.
  Late Jōmon Period.

9 Clay figurine in
  crouched form.
  Late Jōmon Period.

10 Clay figurine with crown-shaped hair. End Jōmon Period.

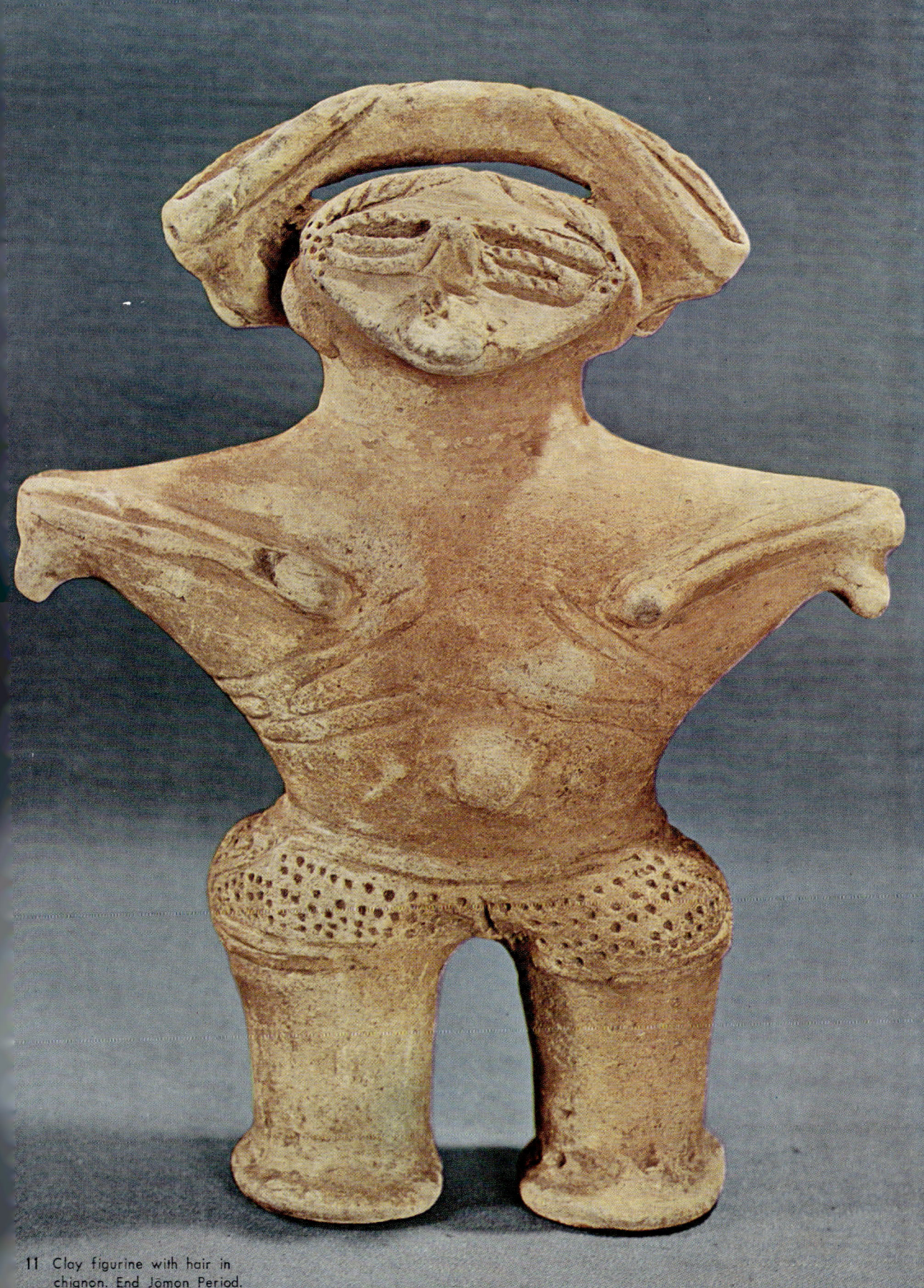
11 Clay figurine with hair in chignon. End Jōmon Period.

12 Jar, red-coloured, Yayoi Type
  Earthenware. Mid-Yayoi Period.

13 Jar, red-coloured, Yayoi Type
  Earthenware. Mid-Yayoi Period.

14 Jar with head, Yayoi Type Earthenware. Mid-Yayoi Period.

15 Clay figurine, inside hollow. Mid-Yayoi Period.

16 *Dōtaku* (bell-shaped bronze) with design of whirlpools. Mid-Yayoi Period.

17 *Dōtaku* (bell-shaped bronze) with design of crossing bands. Late Yayoi Period.

18 Mirror with design of human figures in Chinese type. Mid-Tumuli Period.

19 Gilt-bronze helmet with design of animals. Mid-Tumuli Period.

21 Stone plate with four legs. Mid-Tumuli Period.

20 Horse trappings with design of arabesque. Late Tumuli Period.

22 Figure of woman with crossing bands, *Haniwa*, Late Tumuli Period.

23 Figure of seated man, *Haniwa*, Late Tumuli Period.

24 Figure of water fowl, *Haniwa*. Late Tumuli Period.

25 Figure of bearded man, *Haniwa*. Late Tumuli Period.

26 Jar with decoration, Sue Type Earthenware. Late Tumuli Period.

27 Wall painting with concentric circles. Late Tumuli Period.

28 Wall painting with human figure and horse. Late Tumuli Period.

29 Wall painting with boat. Late Tumuli Period.

1 Urn with stamped patterns. Beginning Jomon Period.

Urn with edges in
shape of mountains.
Early Jōmon Period.

3 Urn, cylinder-Shaped.
   Early Jōmon Period.

4   Bowl with snake handle. Mid-Jōmon Period.

5   Urn with design of stirrups.
    Mid-Jōmon Period.

6 Bowl with whirlpools and oblique lines designs. Late Jōmon Period.

7 Clay vessel with strange holes. Late Jōmon Period.

8 Earthen ear rings. Late and end Jōmon Period.

9 Clay figurine with animal features. Mid-Jōmon Period.

Symbolic clay figurine.
Mid-Jōmon Period.

13 Realistic clay figurine.
Late Jōmon Period.

14 Clay figurine with exaggerated legs. End Jomon Period.

15 Heads of clay figurine. Mid-Jomon Period.

17 Fragment of jar with design of human face.
Jōmon Type Earthenware. End Jōmon Period.

16 Clay figurine with exaggerated nose.
Mid-Jōmon Period.

18 Clay figurine with exaggerated features. End Jōmon Period.

19 Clay figurine with strange features. Mid-Jōmon Period.

20 Clay figurine wearing mask. End Jōmon Period.

21 Clay figurine in shape of vessel. End Jōmon Period.

22 Clay figurine in shape of vessel. End Jōmon Period.

23 Earthen monkey. End Jōmon Period.

24 Jar with design of herring-bones.
Early Yayoi Period.

26 Jar with tall neck, red-coloured. Mid-Yayoi Period.

27 Bowl, red-coloured. Mid-Yayoi Period.

28 Ewer, with openwork. Mid-Yayoi Period.

29 Jar with design of vertical lines. Mid-Yayoi Period.

30 Globular jar. Mid-Yayoi Period.

1 Tall jar. Mid-Yayoi Period.

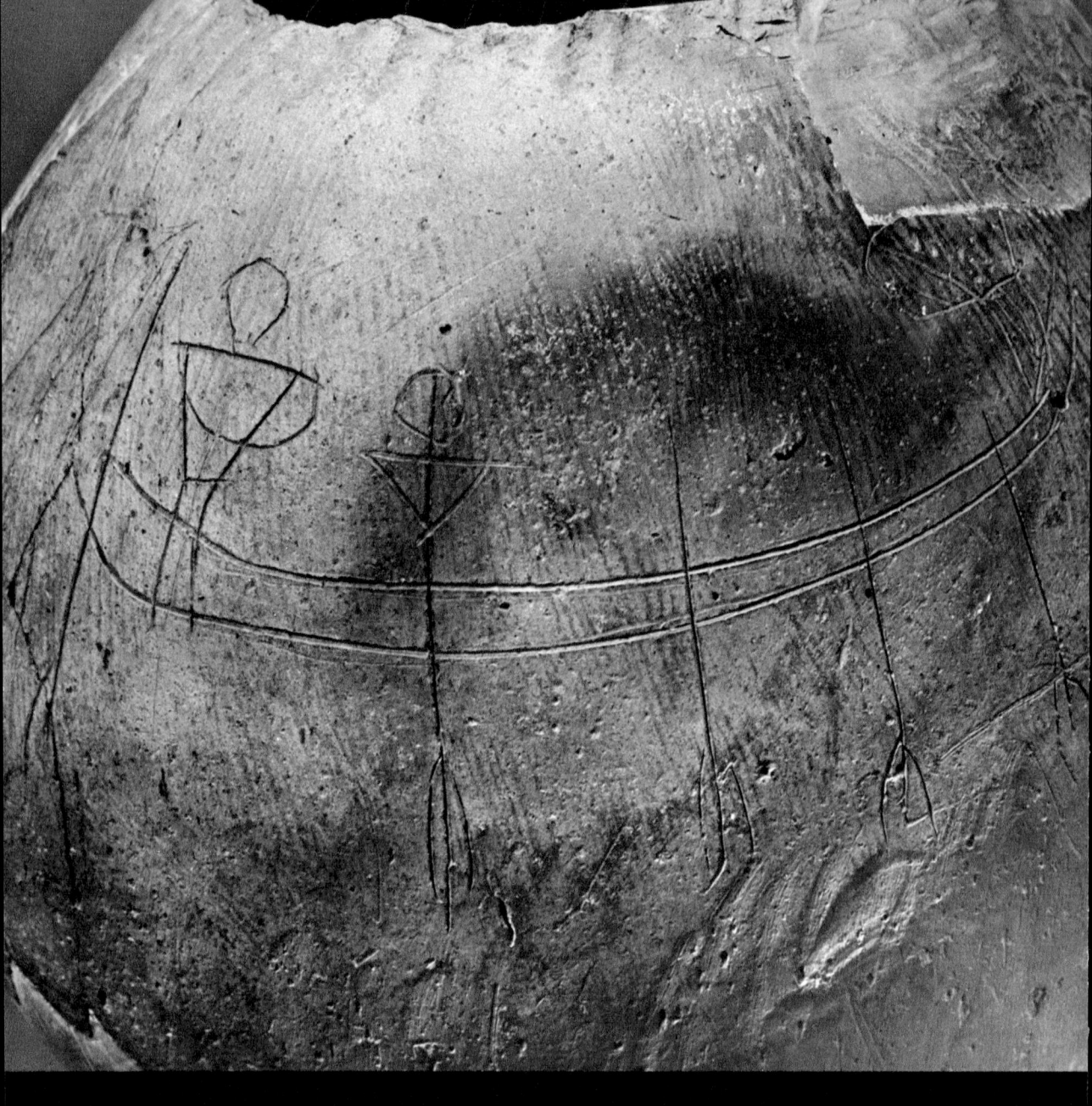
32 "Boating people" on jar. Mid-Yayoi Period.

34 *Dōtaku* (bell-shaped bronze) with deer and water stream designs. Mid-Yayoi Period.

35. *Dōtaku* (bell-shaped bronze) with newt and snap designs. Mid-Yayoi Period.

36 Bronze mirror with design of hunting scenes. Early Tumuli Period

37 Bronze mirror with design of animals. Early Tumuli Period.

38 Figure of large house, *Haniwa*
Mid-Tumuli Period.

39 Figure of boat, *Haniwa*.
Mid-Tumuli Period.

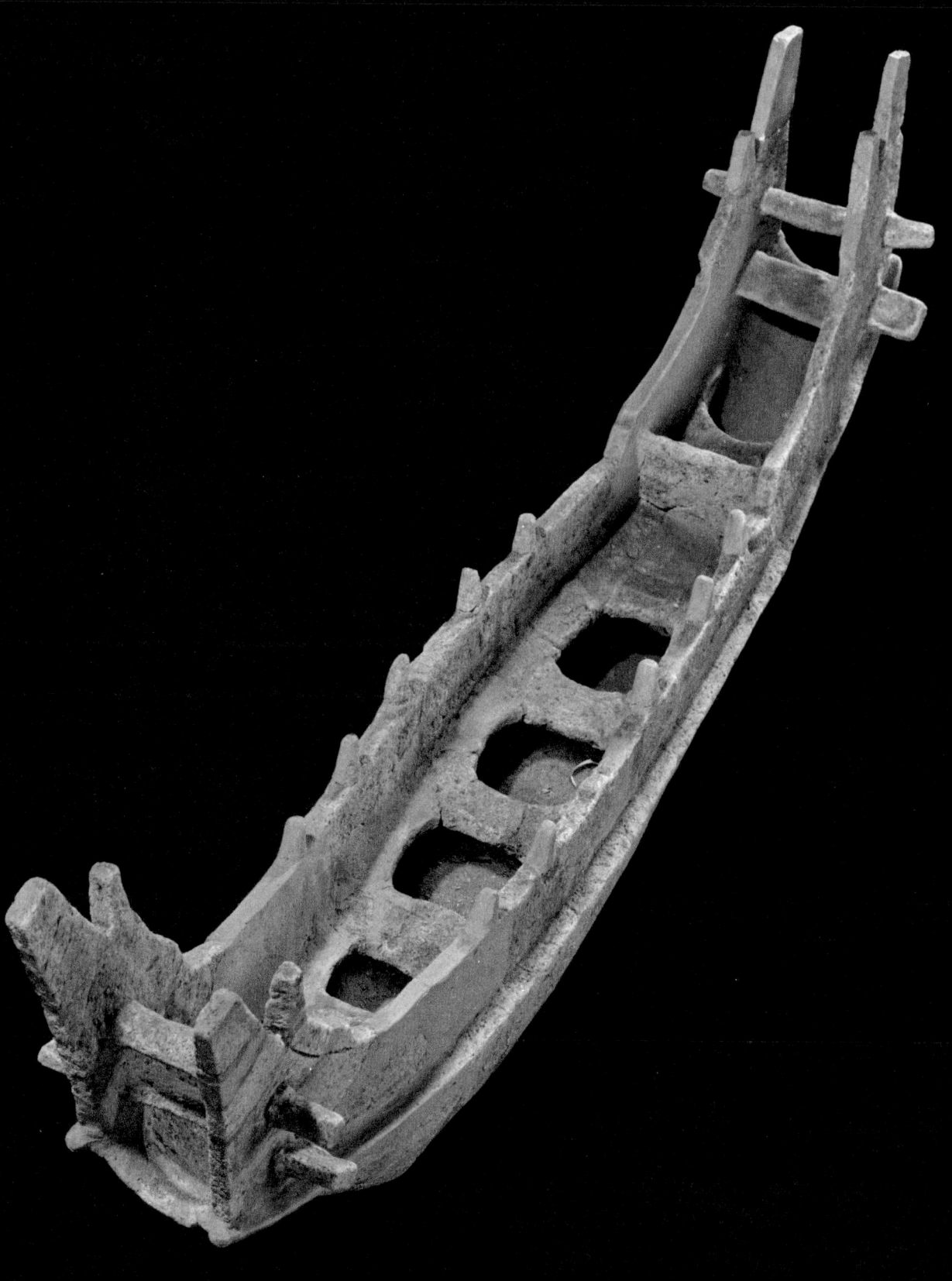

40 Figure of man wearing *Hakama* (trousers form skirt), *Haniwa*. Late Tumuli Period.

41 Figure of woman with hands holding up, *Haniwa*. Late Tumuli Period.

42 Figure of warrior, *Haniwa*. Late Tumuli Period.

43 Figure of man playing Koto (musical instrument), *Haniwa*. Late Tumuli Period.

44 Figure of falcaner, *Haniwa*, Late Tumuli Period.

45 Figure of seated man's face, *Haniwa*. Late Tumuli Period.

Figure of woman, *Haniwa*. Late Tumuli Period.

47 Figure of nurse-maid, *Haniwa*. Late Tumuli Period.

48 Figure of monkey, *Haniwa*.
Late Tumuli Period.

49 Figure of warrior, *Haniwa*
Late Tumuli Period.

50 Figure of wild boar, *Haniwa*.
Late Tumuli Period.

51 Figure of horse with trapping, *Haniwa*.
Late Lumuli Period.

52 Figure of farmer, *Haniwa*. Late Tumuli Period

53 Figure of dancing people *Haniwa*. Late Tumuli Period.

54 Jar on foot decorated human figures, Sue Type Earthenware Late Tumuli Period.

55 A Jar with design of man carrying load on his shoulders.
   B Jar with design of wrestling.

56 Cinerary coffin, pottery, with design of man leading horse in relief carving. Late Tumuli Period.

Asuka & Hakuho Periods

31 Kudara Kannon. Wood. 7th c. Hōryū-ji, Nara.

32 Jikoku Ten. One of Four Guardian Kings. Wood. 7th c. Hōryū-ji, Nara.

33 Yakushi. Bronze. 607 A.D. Hōryū-ji, Nara.

34 Miroku. Wood. 7th c. Kōryū-ji, Kyoto.

35 Bodhisattva (one of "Six Kannon"). Wood. 7th c. Hōryū-ji, Nara.

36 Lady Maya. Bronze. 7th c.
National Museum, Tokyo.

37 Shaka and two attendants. Bronze.
7th~8th c. National Museum, Tokyo.

38 Amida and two attendants, placed in Lady Tachibana's Shrine. Bronze. Late 7th~early 8th c. Hōryū-ji, Nara.

39 Miroku. Clay. Late 7th~early 8th c. Taima-dera, Nara.

41 Relief on pedestal of Yakushi (detail).
Bronze. 7th c. Yakushi-ji, Nara.

40 Head of Yakushi. Bronze.
7th c. Yakushi-ji, Nara.

42 Shaka and two attendants. Stone. Late 7th c. Ishii-dera, Nara.

43 Bodhisattvas, painted on door of Tamamushi Shrine. Color on wood. 7th c. Hōryū-ji, Nara.

44 Jātaka scene on Tamamushi Shrine. Color on wood. 7th c. Hōryū-ji, Nara.

45 Jātaka scene on Tamamushi Shrine. Color on wood. 7th c. Hōryū-ji, Nara.

46 Painting on pedestal of Lady Tachibana's Shrine.
Color on wood. Late 7th–early 8th c. Hōryū-ji, Nara.

47 Painting on pedestal of Lady Tachibana's Shrine. Color on wood. Late 7th – early 8th c. Hōryū-ji, Nara.

49 Heavenly maidens in flight. Mural in Golden Hall. Color on whitewashed wall. Late 7th–early 8th c. Hōryū-ji, Nara.

48 Bodhisattva (Wall No. 2). Mural in Golden Hall. Color on whitewashed wall. Late 7th–early 8th c. Hōryū-ji, Nara.

50 Bodhisattva and attendants (Wall No. 10, detail). Mural in Golden Hall. Late 7th–early 8th c. Hōryū-ji, Nara.

51 Kannon (Wall No. 6 detail). Mural in Golden Hall. Color on whitewashed wall. Late 7th–early 8th c. Hōryū-ji, Nara.

52　Prince Shōtoku. Color on Paper. Late 7th–early 8th c. Imperial Collection.

53　Main Sanctuary (Honden) rebuilt in 1744 A.D. Izumo-taisha, Shimane.

54 Five-storied Pagoda. 7th c.
Hōryū-ji, Nara.

55 Golden Hall (Kondō). 7th c. Hōryū-ji, Nara.

56 Interior of Golden Hall, Hōryū-ji. Nara.

57 Sacred casket, originally installed in the lost pagoda of Sūfuku-ji. Late 7th c. Omi-jingū, Otsu.

58 Gargoyle. Tile. 7th c.
Anonymous collection.

59 Gigaku mask, "Chidō". Wood. 7th c. National Museum, Tokyo.

60 Embroidered picture of Tenjukoku Paradise (detail). Silk. c. 622 A.D. Chugū-ji, Nara.

57 Shaka and two attendants. Bronze. 623 A.D. Hōryū-ji, Nara.

58·59 Kudara Kannon. Wood. 7th c. Hōryū-ji, Nara.

60·61 Guze Kannon. Wood. Early 7 c. Hōryū-ji, Nara

62 Tamon Ten, one of Four Guardian Kings. Wood. 7th c. Hōryū-ji, Nara.

63 Zōjō Ten, one of Four Guardian Kings. Wood. 7th c. Hōryū-ji, Nara.

64 Figure of phoenix attached to canopy.
Wood. 7th c. Hōryū-ji, Nara.

65 Figure of heavenly maiden attached to canopy.
Wood. 7th c. Hōryū-ji, Nara.

66 Yumetagai Kannon. Bronze. Late 7th c. Hōryū-ji, Nara.

67 Bodhisattva (one of "Six Kannon"). W[ood]. Late 7th c. Hōryū-ji, Nara.

68 Scene of Buddha's nirvana. Clay. A.D. 711. Hōryū-ji, Nara.

69 Weeping disciples in the scene of Buddha's nirvana. Clay. 711 A.D. Hōryū-ji, Nara.

70 Weeping disciples in the scene of Buddha's nirvana. Clay. 711 A.D. Hōryū-ji, Nara.

71 Head of Buddha. Bronze. 685 A.D.
Kōfuku-ji, Nara.

72 Woman in the scene of Monju and Yuima in discussion on Buddhism. Clay. 711 A.D. Hōryū-ji, Nara.

73 Miroku. Wood. 7th c. Chūgū-ji, Nara.

74 Bodhisattva, called Kokūzō. Wood. 7th c. Hōrin-ji, Nara.

6 Miroku. Wood. Late 7th c.
Kōryū-ji, Kyoto.

77 Yakushi. Bronze. Late 7th~ early 8th c. Yakushi-ji, Nara.

78 Pedestal of Yakushi. Bronze. Late 7th–early 8th c. Yakushi-ji, Nara.

80 Shō Kannon. Bronze. Late 7th c. Yakushi-ji, Nara.

Top-ornament of East pagoda. Bronze. A.D. 690~730. Yakushi-ji, Nara.

83 Shaka. Bronze. Late 7th– early 8th c. Jindai-ji, Tokyo.

84 Bodhisattva, called Shō Kannon. Wood. Late 7th c. Kinryū-ji, Nara.

85 Lady Maya and heavenly beings. Bronze. 7th c. National Museum, Tokyo.

86 Miroku. Bronze. 7th c. National Museum, Tokyo.

87 · 88 Figures of men. Stone. 7th c. At the tomb of Princess Kibi, Nara.

89 Bodhisattva, painted on door of Lady Tachibana's Shrine. Color on wood. Late 7th~early 8th c. Hōryū-ji, Nara.

90 Kannon (Wall No. 6, detail). Mural in Golden Hall. Color on whitewashed wall. Late 7th~early 8th c. Hōryū-ji, Nara.

91 Bodhisattva (Wall No. 5, detail). Mural in Golden Hall. Color on whitewashed wall. Late 7th~early 8th c. Hōryū-ji, Nara.

92 Amida (Wall No. 6, detail). Mural in Golden Hall. Color on whitewashed wall. Late 7th~early 8th c. Hōryū-ji, Nara.

93 Kannon (Wall No. 3). Mural in Golden Hall. Color on whitewashed wall. Late 7th~early 8th c. Hōryū-ji, Nara.

94 Fun drawing on canopy, heavenly maiden in flight. 7th c. Hōryū-ji, Nara.

95 Fun drawing on ceiling board, boy. 7th c.
    Golden Hall, Hōryū-ji, Nara.

96 Fun drawing on ceiling board, faces of two men.
    7th c. Golden Hall, Hōryū-ji, Nara.

98 Five-storied Pagoda. 7th c. Hōryū-ji, Nara.

99 Inner Main Gateway (Chūmon). 7th c. Hōryū-ji, Nara.

100 Corridor. 7th c. Hōryū-ji, Nara.

101·102 Niō. Clay. 711 A.D. Inner Main Gateway. Hōryū-ji, Nara.

104 Ceiling of East Pagoda. 690~730 A.D.
Yakushi-ji, Nara.

103 Three-storied Pagoda. 7th c. Hokki-ji, Nara.

105 Main Sanctuary (Seiden). Rebuilt in 1953. Kōdai-jingū, Ise.

106 Main Sanctuary (Honden). Rebuilt in 1804. Sumiyoshi-taisha, Osaka.

107·108 Fragments of embroidered picture of Tenjukoku Paradise (detail). Silk. c. 622 A.D. Chūgū-ji, Nara.

109·110 Canopy (detail). Wood. 7th c. Golden Hall, Hōryū-ji, Nara.

111 Figure of heavenly maiden. Relief on tile slab. 8th c. Oka-dera, Nara.

Nara Period

61 Mekira. Clay. 729~48 A.D.
Shin Yakushi-ji, Nara.

62 Gakkō Bosatsu. Clay. First half of 8th c. Tōdai-ji, Nara.

63 Shikkongō Shin. Clay. c. 733 A.D. Tōdai-ji, Nara.

65 Shubodai. Dry-lacquer.
c. 734 A.D. Kōfuku-ji, Nara.

64 Ashura. Dry-lacquer.
c. 734 A.D. Kōfuku-ji, Nara.

66 Priest Gyōshin. Dry-lacquer. 8th c. Hōryū-ji, Nara.

67 Jikoku Ten. Clay. First half of 8th c. Tōdai-ji, Nara.

68 Gigei Ten. Head, Dry-lacquer. Second half of 8th c. Akishino-dera, Nara.

69 Priest Ganjin. Dry-lacquer. c. 763 A.D. Tōshōdai-ji, Nara.

70 Head of Bodhisattva. Dry-lacquer. Second half of 8th c. Tōshōdai-ji, Nara.

71 Gigaku mask, "Karura." Wood. Mid-8th c. Tōdai-ji, Nara.

72 Heavenly musician, on octagonal lantern (detail). Bronze. Mid-8th c. In front of Great Buddha Hall, Tōdai-ji, Nara.

73 Painting on plectrum guard of biwa (lute). Color on leather. 8th c. Shōsō-in, Nara.

74 Bodhisattva painted on pillar. Color on wood. Eizan-ji, Gojō. 763–64 A.D. Octagonal Hall.

75 Shaka Preaching at Vulture Peak (detail). Color on silk. 8th c. Museum of fine arts, Boston.

77 Kichijō Ten. Color on ramie.
c. 772 A.D. Yakushi-ji, Nara.

76 Lady under the tree. Ink and slight color on paper. 8th c. Shōsō-in, Nara.

78 Illustrated Inga-kyō Sutra (detail). Color on paper.
8th c. Jōbonrendai-ji, Kyoto.

79 Sangatsu-dō Hall. 740–50 A.D. Tōdai-ji, Nara.

80 Yume-dono Hall. 8th c. Hōryū-ji, Nara.

81 Yume-dono Hall and surmounting ornament. 8th c. Hōryū-ji, Nara.

82 Interior of Dempō-dō Hall.
730–50 A.D. Hōryū-ji, Nara.

83 Treasure Repository (detail). 750–60 A.D.
Shōsō-in, Nara.

84 Octagonal Hall. 8th c.
Eizan-ji, Gojo.

85 Hand-roll folders.
Knit bamboo. 8th c.
Shōsō-in, Nara.

87 Cloth with design of hunting scene. Silk. 8th c. Shōsō-in, Nara.

86 Ritual banner. Embroidery. 8th c. Shōsō-in, Nara.

88 Mirror. Bronze, lacquered and inlaid. 8th c. Shōsō-in, Nara.

89 Octagonal box, Wood, covered with tortoise shell, with inlay. 8th c. Shōsō-in, Nara.

90 Five-stringed biwa (lute) (detail). Wood with inlay. 8th c. Shōsō-in, Nara.

112 Ashura. Dry-lacquer. c. 734 A.D. Kōfuku-ji, Nara.

113·114 Shubodai. Dry-lacquer. c. 734 A.D. Kōfuku-ji, Nara.

115 Nikkō Bosatsu. Clay. First half of 8th c. Tōdai-ji, Nara.

116 Gakkō Bosatsu. Clay. First half of 8th c. Tōdai-ji, Nara.

117 Kōmoku Ten. Clay. First half of 8th c. Tōdai-ji, Nara.

118 Zōjyō Ten. Clay. First half of 8th c. Tōdai-ji, Nara.

120 Fukū Kensaku Kannon, Nikkō Bosatsu and Gakkō Bosatsu in Sangatsu-do. Tōdai-ji, Nara.

119 Kichijyō Ten. Clay. Second half of 8th c. Tōdai-ji, Nara.

121　Kongō Rikishi. Dry-lacquer. Mid-8th c. Tōdai-ji, Nara.

122　Zōjyō Ten (detail). Dry-lacquer. Mid-8th c. Tōdai-ji, Nara.

123 Anera Taishō. Clay. 729~48 A.D.
Shin Yakushi-ji, Nara.

124 Basara Taishō. Clay. 729~48 A.D.
Shin Yakushi-ji, Nara.

126 Shaka. Dry-lacquer. Second half of 8th c. Saidai-ji, Nara.

125 Eleven-head Kannon. Dry-lacquer. Second half of 8th c. Shōrin-ji, Sakurai.

127 Priest Gyōshin. Dry-lacquer. 8th c. Hōryū-ji, Nara.

128 Nikkō (detail). Dry-lacquer. Second half of 8th c. National Museum, Tokyo.

129 Rushana (detail). Dry-lacquer. c. 759 A.D. Tōshōdai-ji, Nara.

130 Thousand-arm Kannon. Dry-lacquer. Second half of 8th c. Tōshōdai-ji, Nara.

131 Bon Ten. Wood. Second half of 8th c. Tōshōdai-ji, Nara.

132 Taishaku Ten. Wood. Second half of 8th c. Tōshōdai-ji, Nara.

133 Jikoku Ten. Wood. Second half of 8th c. Daian-ji, Nara.

134 Tamon Ten. Wood. Second half of 8th c. Daian-ji, Nara.

135 Gigaku mask, "Suikojyū". Wood. 8th c. Tōdai-ji, Nara.

136 Gigaku mask, "Gojyo". Wood. 8th c. Shōsō-in, Nara.

舉身戰悼不能自持
兩人扶腋在於路側
太子即問此為何人
從者答曰此病人也
太子又問何謂為病
答曰夫謂病者皆由
嗜欲飲食無度四大
不調轉變成病百節
苦痛氣力虛竭飲食
寡少眠臥不安雖有
身手不能自運要假

137 Illustrated Inga-kyō Sutra (detail). Color on paper. 8th c. Jōbonrendai-ji, Kyoto.

138 Lady under the tree (detail). Ink and faint color on paper. 8th c. Shōsō-in, Nara.

139 Lady under the tree (detail). Ink and faint color on paper. 8th c. Shōsō-in, Nara.

140 Bodhisattva (detail). Ink on ramie. 8th c.
Shōsō-in, Nara.

141 Bodhisattva (detail). Color on silk. 8th c.
Shōsō-in, Nara.

142 Design of Sacred animal (detail). Faint color on paper. 8th c. Shōsō-in, Nara.

143 Landscape (detail). Ink on ramie. 8th c. Shōsō-in, Nara.

145 Painting on tray. Litharge color on lacquered wood. 8th c. Shōsō-in, Nara.

144 Birds, painted on tray (detail). Litharge on lacquered wood. 8th c. Shōsō-in, Nara.

146 East Gateway. 8th c.
Hōryū-ji, Nara.

147 Sutra Repository. 8th c.
Hōryū-ji, Nara.

149 Golden Hall. Second half of 8th c.
Tōshōdai-ji, Nara.

148 Lecture Hall. 708–15 A.D.
Tōshōdai-ji, Nara.

150 Crown of Fukū Kensaku Kannon. Silver. c. 746 A.D. Tōdai-ji, Nara.

151 Buddhist ritual banner. Gilt bronze. 8th c. Shōsō-in, Nara.

152 Jar. Silver. 8th c.
Shōsō-in, Nara.

153 Incense burner. Copper. 8th c. Shōsō-in, Nara.

154 Cabinet. Wood. 8th c.
Shōsō-in, Nara.

155 Cabinet. Wood, lacquered. 8th c. Shōsō-in, Nara.

156 Rectangular box. Wood, with marquetry. 8th c. Shōsō-in, Nara.

157 Box. Wood, with gold and silver ornament overlaid with tortoise shell. 8th c. Shōsō-in, Nara.

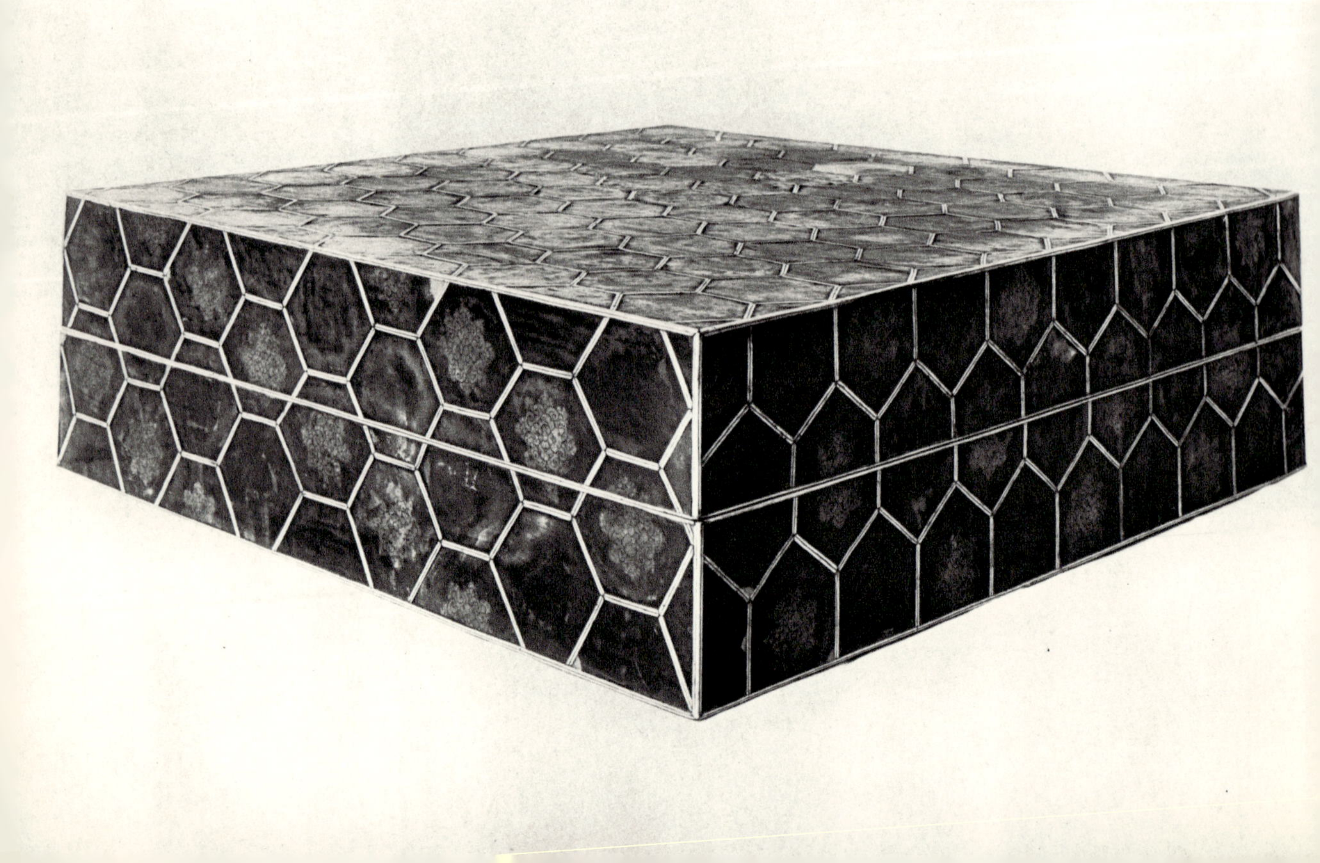

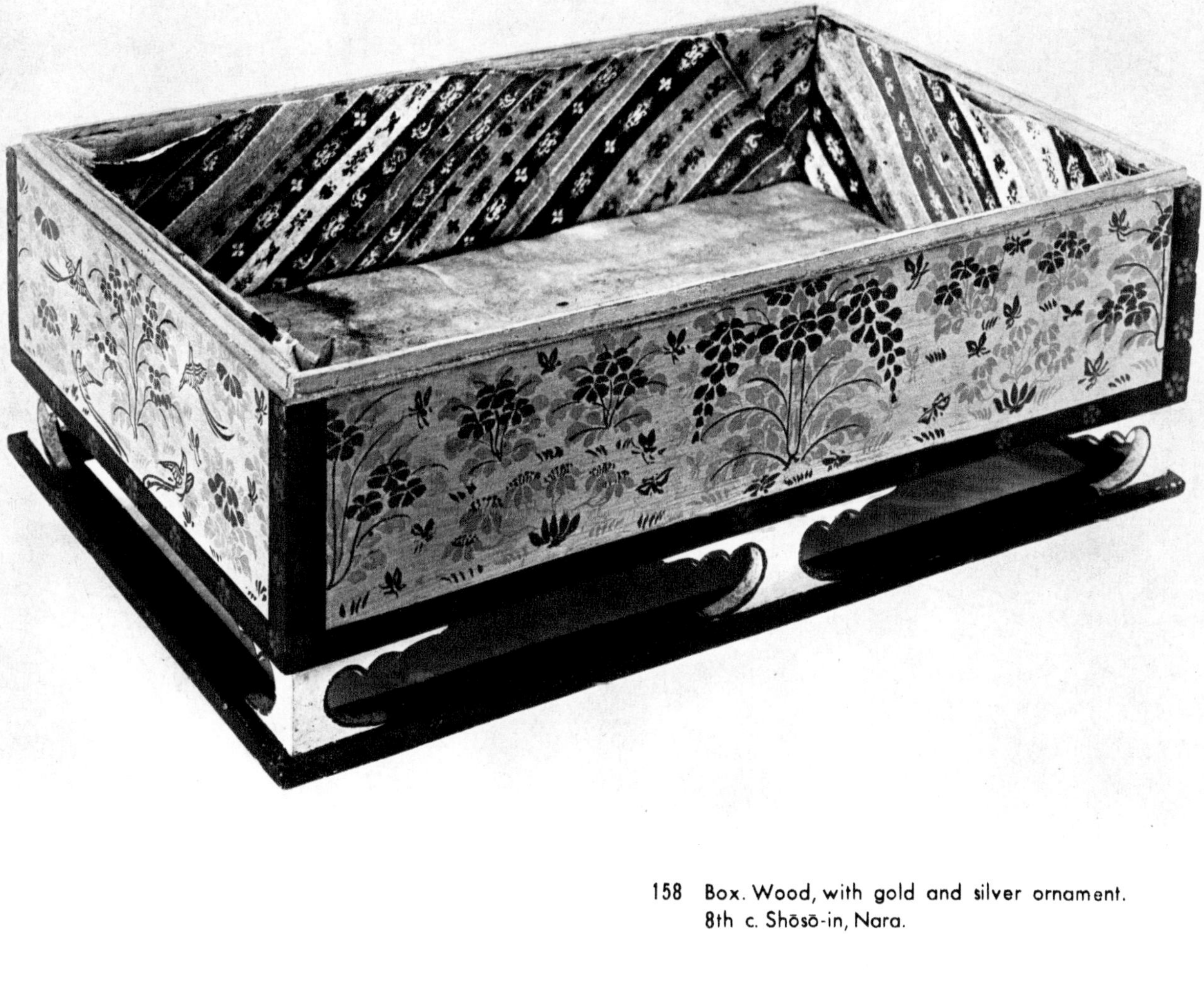

158 Box. Wood, with gold and silver ornament. 8th c. Shōsō-in, Nara.

159 Eight-lobed mirror box. Lacquered hide with gold and silver painting. 8th c. Shōsō-in, Nara.

160 Eight-lobed mirror box. Wood, lacquered, with silver inlay. 8th c. Shōsō-in, Nara.

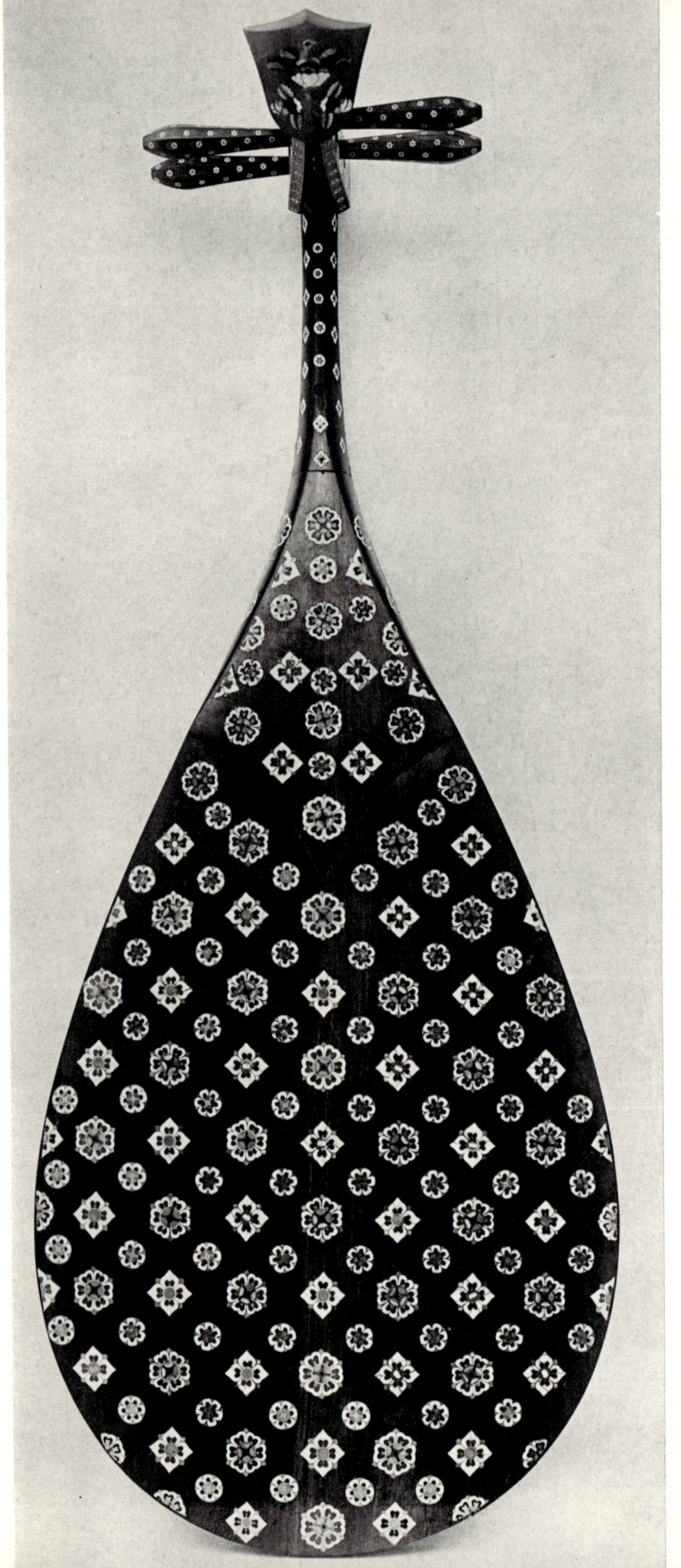

161 Biwa (lute) (back side). Wood, with inlay. 8th c. Shōsō-in, Nara.

162 Foot measures. Green-stained ivory with engravings. Plectrum (*Bachi*, right). Red-stained ivory with engravings. 8th c. Shōsō-in, Nara.

163 Eight-lobed mirror. Bronze, covered with silver. 8th c. Shōsō-in, Nara.

164 Octagonal mirror box. Wood, covered with brocade. 8th c. Shōsō-in, Nara.

165 Bowl. Two-color glazed pottery.
8th c. Shōsō-in, Nara.

167 Vase. Pottery. 8th c.
Shōsō-in, Nara.

166 Dish. Two-color glazed pottery.
8th c. Shōsō-in, Nara.

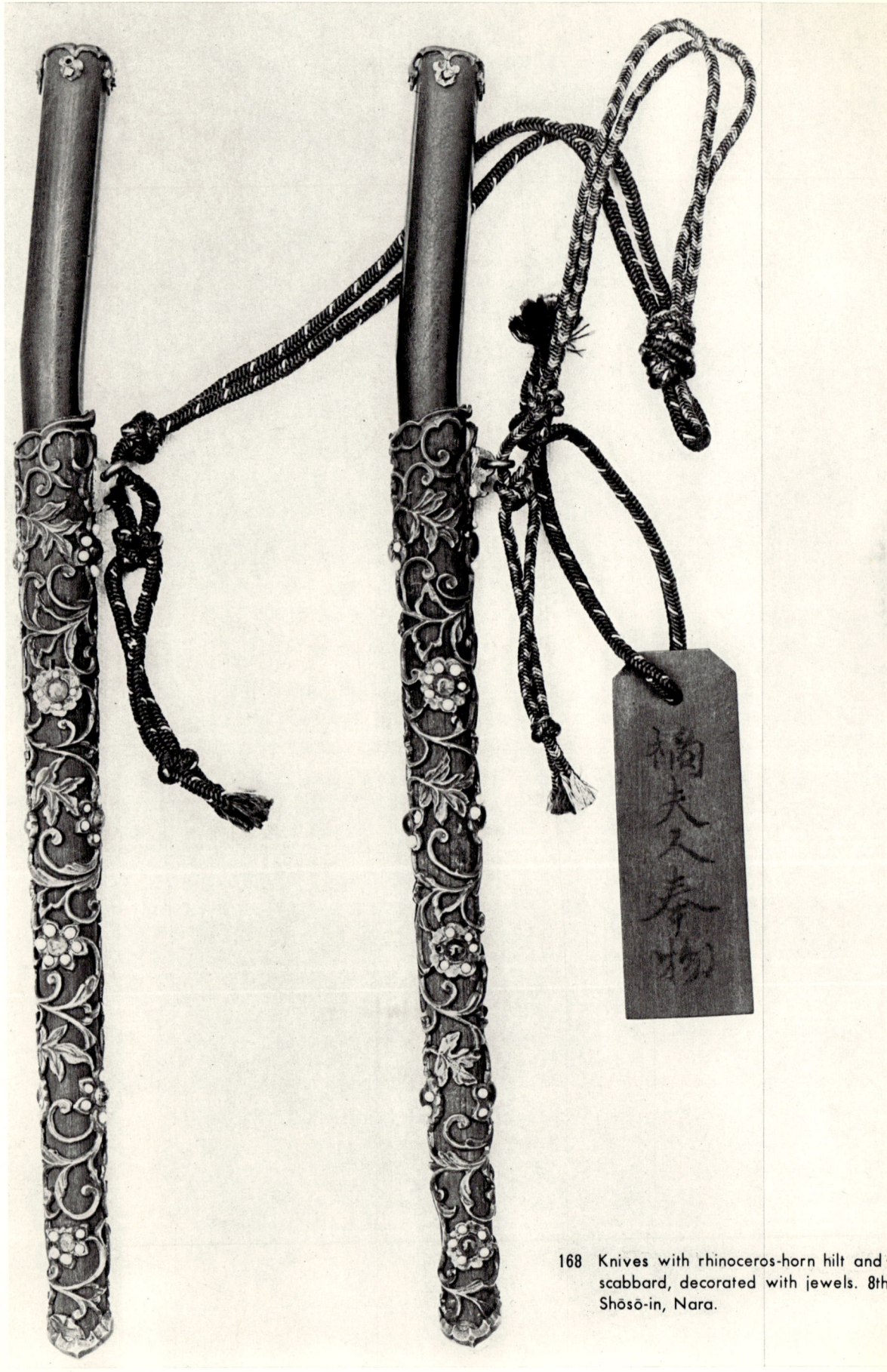

168 Knives with rhinoceros-horn hilt and silver scabbard, decorated with jewels. 8th c. Shōsō-in, Nara.